This is the story of a dream, a dream that began one afternoon in a small apartment when actress Mary Mercier rolled a piece of paper into her typewriter and began to give life to the characters in her imagination. Six hours later emerged the first draft for a play called JOHNNY NO-TRUMP and a dream of a Broadway production. The story of that dream —writing the play, rewriting, finding an agent, finding a producer, getting a director, casting the play, rehearsals, costumes, out-of-town tryouts, building a set, finding a theater, working the lighting, last minute changes —is a long exciting journey, bustling with ideas, people, and hopes of glory. The author held countless interviews with all the people involved and here they tell, mostly in their own words, what they think and feel about JOHNNY NO-TRUMP and their role in it. From typewriter to Broadway opening night, and the breathless waiting for notices, JOHNNY NO-TRUMP is touching, sad, funny and informative, and presents all the scenes behind and in front, in the making of a Broadway play.

ON STAGE

SUSAN JACOBS

The Making of a Broadway Play

ALFRED A. KNOPF  New York

Library of Congress Cataloging in Publication Data

Jacobs, Susan   On stage; the making of a Broadway play.

SUMMARY: Drawing heavily on interviews with the playwright, producers, director, actors, etc., follows the emergence of a Broadway production from writing the play to opening night.

Bibliography: p.
1. Mercier, Mary. Johnny No-Trump—Juvenile literature.
2. Theater—Production and direction—Case studies—Juvenile literature.
1. Theater—Production and direction. 2. Mercier, Mary.
Johnny No-Trump   I. Title   PS3563.E734J635   792.9′097471   74-98893

To Danny

Contents

Cast (in order of appearance)

Harry Armstrong / *Pat Hingle*

Mrs. Franklin / *Barbara Lester*

John Edwards / *Don Scardino*

(Nanna) / *(Anne Ives)*

Florence Edwards / *Sada Thompson*

Alexander Edwards / *James Broderick*

Bettina / *Bernadette Peters*

Acknowledgments. I am especially grateful to the *Johnny No-Trump* company, who were so gracious and informative at a time when they needed no added distractions. In addition, I interviewed a number of people whose names do not appear in the book, but who nonetheless provided valuable information about New York theater. Among them were Melvyn Douglas, Robert Frink, David Hays, Owen Laster, Howard Rosenstone, Diana Sands, Michael Schultz, Bernard Sohn, Leslie Wiener, and Gene Wolsk. My thanks to Ruth Bronz, who got me started on this project, and to my editors: Judy Englehardt, who did the bulk of the editing, Sudi Staub and Carol Hill. Finally, thanks to Marion Carlsen, who babysat.

ON STAGE

Introduction

This book is about the making of a play called *Johnny No-Trump,* written by Mary Mercier and produced on Broadway in the fall of 1967. Although I had acted in repertory theater several years before I began the book, I had no experience on Broadway except as a member of the audience. Nonetheless, I thought I knew what to expect of the Broadway scene. There would be a star, loaded with "temperament" and locking horns constantly with an equally temperamental director. There would be supporting players, each on his own ego-trip. And the playwright would be pacing in the lobby throughout rehearsals, furious with everybody. *Johnny No-Trump,* however, did not fulfill these "show biz" expectations of mine.

As a result, this book tells a different kind of Broadway story: the story of a quest not so much for glory, as for the inside truth about a particular house on Long Island where the play takes place. "It was a matter of reaching her, up around that corner that she kept disappearing around," an actress said of her character in *Johnny No-Trump.* For nearly everyone involved in creating the play it was "a matter of reaching," reaching out, or in, to understand the play, the house, the characters.

As much as possible, the story is told in the words of those who made the play: first the playwright, alone for a long time with her own imaginings; then the producers, who raised the money and hired the people who could embody the characters of the play; the designer, who gave the characters a place to exist in; and finally, the director and the actors, whose imaginations converged during one intense month to bring the play to life on a Broadway stage.

Chapter **1** **The Playwright**

One morning in June, 1967, four months before *Johnny No-Trump* went into rehearsal on Broadway, I went to visit Mary Mercier, the author of the play. Mary was thirty-eight, but as she stood at her door, a very slight figure in faded dungarees, she looked not more than seventeen. She led me into her apartment, furnished "mostly from the Salvation Army," as she put it. In one corner was a mattress on the floor, covered with an Indian spread. In another corner, framed scraps of old tapestries and small memorabilia had been carefully arranged on the wall above a picnic table.

As Mary and I sat facing each other across the picnic table, it seemed at first that she was interviewing me. In a low, probing voice, she asked where I had worked in theater, what writing I had done, and what plays I liked. Her wide blue eyes carefully pondered my answers, and then, just as carefully, considered the questions I asked her about her own career as an actress and playwright.

Mary was born in Wales and had her first taste of the theater at the age of seven, touring with a company that presented plays in Welsh mining towns. In her teens she apprenticed with the Penguin Players outside London, but it was not until she came to the United States at eighteen that her interest in acting solidified. When she arrived in New York City, she began to study drama, while supporting herself with office jobs and as a prop girl backstage.

Always an ardent moviegoer in England, Mary arrived in the United States expecting the country to look like a Hollywood set. "I thought everyone was a millionaire," she said, laughing, "and that there was no such thing as poverty. I thought I must never get off the train in Chicago because I would be gunned down by gangsters. And I thought Billy the Kid was still riding around somewhere out there on the plains."

As an actress, Mary has played off-Broadway and understudied on Broadway. During one summer she acted in two plays at the Spoleto Festival in Italy, and spent another summer touring with Walter Pidgeon in a stock company. She is one of about three hundred members of the Actor's Studio, a renowned drama workshop in New York City, and she considers the work she has done there, acting in scenes and plays, as some of the most stimulating of her career. But Mary is the first to call her career in commercial theater less than sensational. She jokingly told me that the "highlights" of her career were her performances as a "replacement maid" in Chekhov's *The Three Sisters,* and as an extra in a movie called *Greenwich Village.*

Mary's mood became serious as we talked about *Johnny No-Trump,* the first play she had ever written. Every now and then as she spoke, she would lean forward, dark hair swinging around her delicate face, and gesture excitedly with her slender, carefully manicured hands. She recalled first of all a conversation with a fifty-five-year-old actor friend. "We were just talking and he suddenly said to me, 'I have a confession to make. Don't ever tell anyone, but I once wanted to be a poet.' I thought that was extraordinary. I mean it was phrased in such a way that it was a confession! He wasn't proud that he had wanted to be a poet. It was such a secret!"

Although the actor was fifty-five, his "confession" became the basis for sixteen-year-old Johnny, the title character in the play Mary wrote. Like the actor, Johnny's dream is to be a poet.

Another thing that stimulated her imagination as a writer, Mary said, was an incident which occurred at the Actor's Studio. One member, actress Geraldine Page, had just finished a rather over-serious reading of a scene. In the discussion that followed, the Studio's director, Lee Strasberg, said, "Geraldine, someone should write a comedy for you."

Mary recalled, "I thought at the time, *I* could do that! I don't know why I thought I could, but I did. And sitting there at the Studio, a group of characters came into my head. Of course, by the time I got outside and was walking down the street, she had changed—from Geraldine Page, I mean. In the next several months, these characters changed around constantly in my mind. They changed age, nationality, sex, until they became a related group, and when they had formed a group, they began to talk to each other.

"I was on the elevator in Bonwit Teller one day, and I was hearing these characters talking to each other. My former sister-in-law, who was with me, said, 'Mary, where are you?' because my mind was obviously way off somewhere. So I told her that I had these characters in my head, and she said, 'Why don't you try writing them down?' "

That night at her apartment Mary began. "When I sat down to write I saw the central character, Harry, sitting in the middle of the stage, and all of a sudden it started to rain. I thought, 'All right, I'll go along with that.' Then a character I'd never seen before, Mrs. Franklin, a neighbor, came through the door and said, 'Well, I'm here.' That seemed as good a beginning as any, so I wrote it down."

Six hours later, Mary Mercier had finished most of the first act of the play. "I was so astonished that I put it away. It scared me, that I'd written it so fast. It scared me because everybody thinks he can write a play."

Six hours does seem a surprisingly short time in which to write a first act, but more experienced playwrights have said they, too, write their plays quickly. Playwright Arthur Miller wrote the whole of *Death of a Salesman* in five or six weeks. And Edward Albee has said that his actual writing time is "very short, anywhere from a month to three months." Both Miller and Albee emphasized, however, that the idea for a play takes time to develop in their minds, and it is sometimes years before they begin to put pen to paper.

There had been a period of about nine months between the time the characters first came to mind and the day Mary Mercier sat down and wrote out the first act. Another month passed before she reread it, "to see if it looked actable." She was fairly satisfied, and began the second act. But this time the writing didn't go so quickly, partly because Mary was working at the same time as an actress.

Nevertheless, what began as the story of one family rapidly grew at Mary's typewriter into an entire town. "At some point, all the people on the block came in, especially in the second act, to wish Johnny a happy birthday. Each of them was a complete person. Each one of those people could have had a play of his own. They were all in the play when I first wrote it, but then I had to cut them out, because, well, a very large cast like that is impractical. It does put people off producing the play." (The high cost of producing on Broadway usually makes large casts—and the resulting large payrolls—economically unfeasible.)

Mary continued, "I cut out a lot of things. One tiny little character got dropped out of the play even though she had already been formed inside me as a character. But she is, unfortunately, rather strong, and now she's demanding her own play. She feels that she has been brought to life and now is neither real nor fictional, but hangs in mid-air.

"I wrote virtually without a plan," Mary added. "The people became so real to me that in a way it was as if they were telling me what to write, and I was merely their typist. If they had wanted to go off on a tangent, they would have won.

"And then sometimes I had to leave the play for a while, because from time to time I would get acting jobs. But the characters made me go back to the play. They made me go on until it was finished. Whatever play this is going to be, it's theirs."

Mary's sense of being taken over by her characters is an experience that has been described by other playwrights. The Italian playwright Luigi Pirandello wrote *Six Characters in Search of an Author* when he found his characters "before me, alive—you could almost touch them and even hear them breathe." Pirandello didn't want to write a play about them, but "these six were already living a life which was their own and not mine any more, a life which was not in my power any more to deny them."

I asked Mary Mercier if there was anything of her own childhood in *Johnny No-Trump*'s plot, which revolves around the conflict between a rebellious sixteen-year-old and his elders. "No," she answered, "the play isn't autobiographical at all. I can write about imaginary characters, but so far I haven't the courage required to write about my own past."

Mary conceded, however, that some experiences with American families in the recent past had affected her play. "Originally," she told me, "this play took place in Staten Island. I used to visit a family there and I liked its strange atmosphere of not belonging to this world." Mary also visited Long Island, where she met a family who had lived in the same house for generations, like the family in *Johnny No-Trump*. Ultimately, she chose the Long Island setting for her play.

Though Mary had kept a diary since age seven, and certainly had the raw material for a play about her own adolescence, young Johnny in the play is in an entirely different situation than Mary had been as a teenager. Mary's upbringing was taken over from her parents by an aunt at age seven, and during the war she lived with a number of foster families. "Each family had a different religion and a different outlook," she said. "You can imagine with all that, that I was a pretty mixed-up kid."

Perhaps the play Mary has written is, instead, an answer or counterpoint to her own experiences as a teenager. For in *Johnny No-Trump,* as Mary wrote in her introduction to the play, "Nearly all the people . . . love each other, and no matter what they ask of one another, it is all done in the name of love rather than anything else."

Chapter 2 The Play

The following summary of Mary Mercier's play, *Johnny No-Trump,* is in two parts: first, a description of each character in the play, and second, a synopsis of the play itself.

The Characters

Nanna. Nanna is Johnny's grandmother, a spirited old lady who has lived most of her life in the old Long Island house where the play takes place. The playwright tells us that she particularly admires a pioneer ancestor who "fought snakes in the desert . . . looked coyotes straight in the eye," and walked all the way to California.

Harry Armstrong. Harry is Johnny's uncle, a retired cab driver in his sixties. He first went to work at fourteen, and has spent most of his life struggling to make ends meet. As a result, he tends to equate happiness with money in the bank. "That man came through the depression," another character says of him, "and that's why he knows the price of everything and that's about all." Harry talks like a tough New York cabbie, but underneath the rough surface he is a loving man, devoted to his mother, Nanna, and deeply concerned for his nephew, Johnny. He is a bachelor.

Florence Edwards.   Florence is Johnny's mother. She has been divorced from his father since Johnny was a baby. Unlike her older brother, Harry, Florence managed to get an education, and she is now a school-teacher. She believes that she and Johnny have an honest relationship, but as the play unfolds, she learns that her son doesn't agree.

Johnny Edwards.   Johnny is a sixteen-year-old boy, throwing all of his considerable energy into "finding" himself. The script says he is "short, thin, wears glasses, and has an odd look to him." He hasn't much interest in sports, and his interest in girls (a word he pronounces with contempt) is well-disguised. Nor does he care about school: teachers are a bore, he claims, and "whole chunks of me are dropping dead." What Johnny does care about passionately is poetry. He loves reading it, and also tries to write his own, scribbling for hours in a notebook. He tells his mother that poetry is the only thing in life that makes him feel special.

Alec Edwards.   Alec is Johnny's father and Florence's ex-husband. He no longer lives in the Long Island house, but comes to visit on special occasions. By profession he is a painter. He drinks heavily, perhaps because, though devoted to his art, he is a failure professionally. At forty-one, he is still obliged at times to borrow rent money.

Bettina.   The playwright calls this young girl who lives next door "a very grown-up fifteen." Bettina's parents, like Johnny's, are divorced. She is a showoff, trying to act sophisticated, and constantly bragging about her clothes, her many boyfriends, and her plans to study at "the University of Paris—in France."

Mrs. Franklin.   An elderly next-door neighbor, Mrs. Franklin runs a sort of boarding house, and to make extra money, also cleans Johnny's house and cares for his grandmother. Harry says of Mrs. Franklin that she has "got fifty cents of every dollar that ever came her way." She appears on stage only briefly, grumbling every time.

The Action

Act One, Scene One. The curtain rises. It is a rainy Saturday morning in February. Harry is alone on the stage, but soon after, Johnny comes downstairs into the living room, wearing pajamas.

"This is gonna be a quiet day," Harry observes, but Johnny quickly teases him into an argument. They bicker playfully for a while, but then their argument becomes serious, as Harry asks Johnny, "What the hell you gonna be? . . . Whatcha gonna do when it comes time to put on a shirt and collar and act responsible?"

Reluctantly, Johnny confesses that he wants to be a poet. This sets Harry off on a tirade. Poetry isn't practical: "Who the hell buys poems for God's sake?" And it's not masculine: "Stay away from them *feminine kinda jobs!*" The attack winds up with a remark about Johnny's father, the unsuccessful painter: "Take a good gander at your old man . . ." Johnny falls silent.

After a while, Harry feels guilty, and asks his nephew to "read me one of your bits." Johnny is afraid Harry will misunderstand and make fun of his poetry, but eventually he reads aloud a poem called "Someday."

When Harry hears "Someday," it suddenly occurs to him that Johnny could be a poet and earn a living too. "You . . . could be . . . a songwriter," he advises cheerfully. "Write words for the *top ten*." And he begins to sing "Someday" in cha-cha rhythm.

Johnny is furious, though for a moment he sings along. But when Harry concludes by telling him to "take a walk," Johnny, still in pajamas, angrily runs outside into the pouring rain. Seconds later he tears back in and up the stairs, shouting "Mother's coming!"

Florence enters, carrying Johnny's wet pajama top, which he had torn off in his fury. She sees that Harry is about to explode, and tells him to "relax and take things in stride in your old age." Harry moans back, "What the hell did I wanna retire for?" After working for forty-six years, he complains, all he gets is "aggravation and nervousness."

Curtain.

Act One, Scene Two. Forty-five minutes later, Harry and Florence are having lunch together at the dining room table. Harry doesn't tell Florence that Johnny wants to be a poet, but he lets Florence know in other ways that he thinks Johnny is an oddball. He ventures the opinion that Johnny has "no trumps."

Florence comes angrily to her son's defense, calling Harry "a fat ignoramus, and an old fart into the bargain." This sends him off to the basement to watch a football game, but not before an angry retort: "And one more thing strikes me funny. How my goin' out to work, me bein' so ignorant and all, and goin' out to slog, made it possible for you to get fancy, and not exactly walk alongside of us no more. Now there must be a joke there, if it would only come to me."

Their conversation has set Florence thinking. When Johnny comes downstairs for lunch, she asks him, "What do you really want out of this world, Johnny?"

At first he says he wants "a loose healthy immoral life like everybody else." Then, to "strike life, like some guy strikes oil." Finally, he opens up to his mother and blurts out, "I'd like to quit school so I can learn something, get a job, then write verse!"

Florence dismisses him: "Would you please get lost!" But when Johnny will not let the subject drop, she gets angry. "Harry's right," she says, "you're getting very fresh." After a moment, however, she calms down, and asks Johnny to tell her about his poetry. He shows her his notebook, and she remarks, "It's all very sweet, Johnny, but do this alongside your education."

As tempers rise again, Florence reveals her deep fear that Johnny may grow up to be like his father. "Your father got stuck with the desire to paint. He's in love with a way of life, an Art, that just doesn't love him back," she says.

Johnny finally becomes desperate. Suddenly, holding up his note-book, he shouts that his poetry is "garbage," that it "really belongs buried! In the garden!" and runs out of the front door to bury it.

Florence's pleas to "unbury it" are in vain. Johnny calls back, "I ain't playin' no game where I don't like the ground rules! We just parted company, Ma!" Then he runs back in, up the stairs, and slams the door to his room.

The commotion rouses Harry from the basement. "The ship is headed for the rocks," he comments, and then returns to the basement, slamming the door behind him. Florence slams the front door, and the curtain falls.

Act Two.   It is the next day after lunch. As the curtain rises, Harry is whipping cream for Johnny's birthday party, which is planned for four o'clock that afternoon. Johnny is also on stage, piling things in a suit-case. He isn't planning to come to his birthday party. "I'm leaving . . . just *zip,* out the door, off."

Harry answers calmly, "So, I've just spent an hour makin' this Creamo Whippo for no reason? You won't be at the party?" But when he sees Johnny packing the family silver into the suitcase, he explodes. "Shakespeare! You're another Murf the Surf!"

They are exchanging threats as Johnny's father, Alec, enters. The moment Harry sees Alec, he begins to criticize him. Alec looks "a wreck," his "cuffs are frayed," he has lost weight. When Alec tells them he is about to have a one-man show of his paintings, Harry advises, "Try not to screw it up. Don't worry, you'll screw it up." Alec would like a drink, but Harry fixes him a sandwich instead.

At Florence's request, Alec has come early to talk with Johnny about his future. He is just about to broach the subject of the poetry when Bettina makes a dramatic entrance from next door.

Johnny looks up. "Cake's at four. This is two-thirty," he says, making it clear he doesn't welcome her presence. But Bettina ignores him, and begins flirting with Alec. Johnny continues to taunt her until she punches him in the ribs, and then a battle is on. It takes Florence to separate the two of them and force a grudging "sorry" out of Johnny. Bettina leaves.

Florence turns to Johnny, telling him that he should be more understanding, for Bettina is only a "glossy dead little girl who pretends she's got a date every Saturday night." Johnny answers, "How dare you understand a stranger and not me!"

Hurt, and wanting to speak privately with Alec, Florence asks Johnny to go to the store for some bread. Johnny refuses. Angrily, his mother slaps him, and he challenges her to slap him again, "if you wanna hurt me." She does, twice more, before her anger turns to sadness.

She wonders aloud what would happen if Johnny really did run away from home. What would he think of his family? "You wouldn't care for them much, they're so ordinary. Always a fight over this and that—not much style to them, no manners, no affection, no tenderness, not particularly honest. Never done anything fine or beautiful in their whole lives." Florence gets her coat to go for the bread herself. "I'm sorry I hit you, baby . . . I'll never do it again," she says as she leaves.

Now Johnny reproaches himself for not being able to show his mother how he feels about her. "I can write in a book, 'You are the eye and sky of my heart,' but I can't just walk across the room and say 'I love you.'" He turns to Alec and Harry. "Hope you guys all know what a *man* is, cos if you don't, and I don't . . . ha ha ha."

Harry and Alec offer him their views about what it means to be a man. But Johnny doesn't seem to trust Alec on this subject. "Why'd you marry my mother?" he demands. Alec answers that he loved Johnny's mother, but "I paid the real attention to my work, and so she closed off." And he concludes, "I regret that we're not father and son."

"My father, my dad is Uncle Harry, and could never be anybody else," Johnny tells him.

Still wanting to help, Alec offers to dig up the "entire front yard," if necessary, to find Johnny's poetry notebook. But Harry stops him, for he has seen Johnny hide the poetry under his sweater, and knows he hasn't really buried it. With scarcely a pause, Harry launches into a sales pitch. "Alexander, you see this kid sitting here . . . This kid sitting here . . .

is a *fantastic* talent." Harry waxes poetic in his praise, asking Alec to put up five dollars to hear "beautiful words comin' at you," and telling Johnny, "Get out that poem! *You're makin' your first sale!*" Harry puts down two dollars himself.

The topic of money reminds Alec that he is short of cash, and he asks for a fifty-dollar loan. This doesn't fluster Harry, but he is brought to a jarring halt when Johnny announces that he has decided not to be a poet. "Poetry is very hard . . . you have to be born with it . . . and be sensitive . . . I'm really just another crawly kid."

Now Harry makes a proposal. He had planned to give Johnny a transistor radio for his birthday, but Johnny had told him he didn't want it. So Harry will either take the radio back to the store and give Johnny the $149 it cost, or he will give Johnny his trust. Johnny has to choose. "Ya want the money? . . . Or my faith?"

It is a difficult decision for Johnny. "No way I can get both, is there?" Finally he chooses Harry's trust, and the two shake hands warmly on their deal.

Alec calls for a poem and Johnny recites one dedicated to his mother:

If the sun shines not,
Would you dawn the day for me?
If the moon rides not,
Will you light the night?
Or honor the spark, in the dark, that hides
Inside your son, who shines not, nor rides.

"You don't have to like it," Johnny says breathlessly when he finishes. "I mean, did you hate it?"

Alec smiles. "No. No."

Harry is euphoric. He proposes drinks and cigars. Catching sight of the birthday cake, he says, "Let's have a private party. Let's cut the cake." So they light the candles and put on party hats. Even Alec, who has his drink at last, is merry. Johnny, cigar in hand, recites another poem, this one about himself, and then still another, dedicated to Harry.

Just then Bettina dashes in. "Some kid's taking your bike apart down the block," she shouts to Johnny. He runs out, and she turns to the others to tell them why she really came. Johnny's mother has been hit by a truck. She is dead.

Harry is staggered: "That couldn't be true—she was just standin' there—she just went for bread, that's all." But a call from the hospital confirms it. Alec leaves to identify the body, telling Harry, "Stay and take care of your kid."

When Johnny returns, still full of party spirit, Harry tells him the news. "John, your mother's dead. Wish I had a real gift of the gab, and could put it to you exactly right and proper, and it wouldn't come out blunt. And if it came out that way, then I meant for it to be different."

At first Johnny can't believe it. "Oh . . . I should have gone for the bread . . . I'll do what she wants. Everything she wants. I'll do what you all want." Suddenly he pulls his poetry book from under his sweater and starts to tear it up.

Harry says, "Gimme the book. Trust me."

Johnny tells Harry, "You mustn't get upset, you hear. You worry too much. That's all you do. You sit around and worry. Nothing's wrong. We're gonna be all right . . ."

Curtain.

Chapter **3** **Agents and Producers: Selling the Play**

Roughly two years after Mary Mercier began to write *Johnny No-Trump,* she showed her manuscript to two friends, who offered suggestions that led her to rewrite the ending. The script was in final form by April 1965, but since Mary had no money to have it professionally typed, she had to do it herself. Several other friends saw it then, but only one, an unemployed actor, had anything positive to say.

The play was offered to, and rejected by the Herbert Berghof Studio and the Actor's Studio, whose members sometimes do workshop productions of new plays, and the American Place Theater, which presents the work of new playwrights to paying audiences. Meanwhile, the agent who represented Mary as an actress liked *Johnny No-Trump,* and offered to represent Mary as playwright also. But according to Mary, the play was only sent "to two people, maybe one. For a year I was under the impression that the script was being sent to people and it wasn't."

By chance, sometime in the spring of 1966, Mary mentioned to a director at the Actor's Studio that she had written a play. It was on his recommendation that literary agent Bertha Case read *Johnny No-Trump.*

Bertha Case is one of about a hundred literary agents in New York.

If an agent reads and likes a manuscript, he or she will try to sell it, usually for a commission of ten percent, to a producer, book publisher, magazine, etc. If a sale is made, the agent then arranges contract terms on behalf of the author.

Some agents represent all kinds of writers, but a few specialize in playwrights. In the latter case, it is the agent's business to know about various producers and directors, and to have an idea of the kinds of plays they are looking for. The agent is also responsible for any subsidiary rights; that is, the sale of the play abroad, or to the movies, or to a publishing company if it is to appear in book form.

For all these reasons, most playwrights find a good agent very helpful. Mary Mercier's experience with *Johnny No-Trump* is an excellent example. Within weeks after Bertha Case agreed to represent *Johnny No-Trump,* it was sold to a Broadway producer.

I first spoke with Bertha Case about *Johnny No-Trump* one afternoon in August at Miss Case's business office on Fifty-third Street in New York City. Miss Case is a handsome woman in her sixties, and greeted me from behind an awesome executive desk. She has a husky voice, and being French-born, speaks with a slight accent.

Around the walls of the office were posters of productions whose playwrights she had represented, and photographs of clients and friends. Among the photos was one of the German singer and actress Lotte Lenya, as she appeared in the title role of Bertolt Brecht's play, *Mother Courage.* It is inscribed, "For Bertha, with all my love."

Miss Case told me that it was at the Long Island home of her friend Lotte Lenya that she first read Mary Mercier's play. She explained that she often brought along scripts she was considering when she visited Miss Lenya. "They were used to seeing me read through a play and say, 'This is garbage, terrible.' "

On the evening Bertha Case read *Johnny No-Trump,* Lotte Lenya was giving a cocktail party. Miss Case was reading the play "in my bathing suit or something," when guests began to arrive, and Miss Lenya asked if she would like to go upstairs and change. Reluctantly, she did. But she returned quickly and continued to read, looking up only briefly as more guests arrived.

"Lenya was handing me a martini, when I looked up at her with tears in my eyes. She said, 'Bertha, you must have gotten a fly in your eye or something. You can't be moved by a *play!*' And I said, 'I am moved by this play.' "

The next day, Miss Case telephoned Mary Mercier and told her how much she liked *Johnny No-Trump*. Then, with Mary's consent, she arranged to have Mary's single battered manuscript professionally typed. Once this was done, she telephoned five producers and told them about the play. "They all sent messengers for it," Miss Case laughed, "because I raved so about it."

The first producer to respond had "crazy ideas about changing the play, so we felt he really wasn't our man." Then a producer named Richard Barr called. "He wanted to buy it instantly, so I called the others to find out their reactions." Two other producers, Kermit Bloomgarten and Herman Shumlin, also liked the play and wanted to buy it. The fifth, David Susskind, didn't like it. "Meanwhile," Bertha Case says, "Dick Barr was calling and calling, and we couldn't hold the play any longer, so we sold it to him."

The terms of her contract provided that Mary Mercier would receive one thousand dollars as an advance against ten percent royalties, that is, ten percent of the producer's profits. The contract did not guarantee, however, that the play would ever be produced on stage, for all a producer actually buys when he signs is an option, which gives him exclusive rights to the play for a certain period of time. Richard Barr and two co-producers, Clinton Wilder and Charles Woodward, Jr., optioned *Johnny No-Trump* for the 1966–1967 theater season. Because of difficulties in assembling a company, however, their option was renewed, and plans were made to go into rehearsal in the fall of 1967.

About a month before rehearsals were to begin, I went to see Richard Barr, a young-looking fifty-year-old with a booming voice, confident stride and vigorous handshake, at his office in the Broadway theater district. I asked him why he had chosen to produce *Johnny No-Trump*.

"In the first place, Mary's play was written with a complete freshness," Barr said. "By that, I mean there were very few, if any, clichés in the relationships of the characters. The use of the English language was remarkable for a playwright—you really look for that. Mary writes beautiful English and seems to use the right words for her characters. The characters jump off the page. There are marvelous people in this play. Further, she has a very modern point of view about the younger generation, which is non-hippy and also isn't sentimental. It's a very strong point of view, and the young man is a very attractive sixteen-year-old and that appealed to us a great deal. Then of course the natural humor that was in it—there's some very funny stuff and very tender stuff, and the whole thing just added up. She really sat down and wrote what she set out to do, and we thought it would be just fine.

"Mary's play simply came across my desk," Barr continued, indicating a long table in front of him crowded with stacks of scripts, loose papers and a pushbutton telephone. "I read about fifteen plays a week (I've read over three thousand now), and it was one of the fifteen which I happened to read. I immediately sent it to Wilder, who was in the country, and he liked it as well as I did, and we bought it. Right away."

The decision to produce *Johnny No-Trump* on Broadway, rather than off-Broadway, was a departure for Barr and Wilder. They had been producing the work of new young playwrights mostly off-Broadway for some time. "Off-Broadway" refers to a cluster of small theaters that grew up, mainly in downtown New York, in the 1950s, when many creative theater people began to look outside the ten-block Broadway district to find a forum for cheaper, more experimental theater. In 1959, because he was "fairly fed up" with the expenses on Broadway, Barr had gone off-Broadway, too. He felt "there was a great deal of freedom off-Broadway and that one could really return the theater to the playwright."

At that time he was lucky enough to discover the then-unknown Edward Albee, whom some now consider this country's major playwright. Barr produced Albee's first play, *The Zoo Story,* off-Broadway in a double bill with *Krapp's Last Tape,* by the avant-garde playwright Samuel Beckett, and together the two plays ran 582 performances, the longest-running non-musical in off-Broadway history. Then he and Clinton Wilder co-produced Albee's *The American Dream* and *The Death of Bessie Smith.* Albee himself was asked to become a member of the producing team in 1962, and a new partnership of Albee, Barr, and Wilder, called ABW Productions, was cemented.

By producing off-Broadway, and cutting such costs as set design, lighting, costumes, and salaries to a bare minimum, ABW Productions has since been able to introduce a number of new talents. Jack Richardson's *Gallows Humor,* for example, was staged for four thousand dollars. "Our basic rule," Barr said in 1961, "is never to spend a nickel where we can use imagination and ingenuity instead."

Up to now, however, Edward Albee was the only playwright ABW had brought to Broadway, and so they were taking a risk in producing an unknown like Mary Mercier. Her "voice" as a playwright was quite different from Edward Albee's, softer and less strident.

But perhaps the extent of ABW's gamble on *Johnny No-Trump* can best be understood if the complexities of producing a Broadway show are explained. First, of course, the producers must raise the money to finance the production. On Broadway this may run from $75,000 to $300,000 or more for a non-musical. As the largest share of funds usually comes from investors, producers have to keep them in mind when selecting a play, choosing one they will think is worth gambling on. Experienced producers with a good record of successes are likely to have a pool of backers willing to put up money largely on the basis of the producer's endorsement. A long-time investor in ABW's productions, for example, says, "The play itself means maybe forty percent to me. The weight I put on the script is subordinate to the weight I put on who is producing it."

In at least one case, the reputation of the producer alone, regardless of the script, is enough to attract backers. Harold Prince, a producer with a spectacular record of successful musicals, doesn't even permit his backers to read the book (as the script is called), or hear the musical score before they invest. "Why should I?" he asks. "I don't understand how my car works, so I never make mechanics show me the engine. I wouldn't know what I was looking at anyway. So I see no reason to show investors how the show looks or sounds." Investors in his productions have little reason to doubt his judgment. Someone who invested $1,000 in his production of the musical *Pajama Game* in 1954, and then let his money ride on subsequent productions, *West Side Story, Fiddler on the Roof,* and *Cabaret,* would have earned $30,000 by 1967.

After a Broadway producer has the capital in hand, or perhaps even before, he begins to look for the best possible director for the play, and to think about casting, a responsibility he usually shares with the director and playwright. To do this, he needs to know the theater scene intimately. Inevitably, too, there will be hitches. The director he likes may not like the play, while another director who likes the play may not have time to do it. Then, perhaps, an actor that the director and producer particularly want to hire may not be available. Or a star may ask a prohibitive salary.

The producer is also responsible for booking a theater. This may involve lengthy negotiations, since theater owners have a large stake in the play's success. They receive enough to cover their expenses (which include the salaries of the house staff, certain technicians, and some advertising costs) while a play runs. But only if the play is a hit does a theater owner make a substantial profit. The agreement with the producer usually stipulates that the theater owner will receive thirty percent of the gross receipts until they reach $25,000 to $30,000 a week, and twenty-five percent thereafter. So theater owners want to book plays with commercial possibilities, and they will usually ask to see a script; they also tend to be more receptive if a star is cast in a leading role.

Once the theater is booked, and a cast and director have assembled on stage to begin rehearsals, the producer can breathe a large sigh of relief. But he will not leave New York for a vacation, for in addition to his administrative duties during the rehearsal period, a producer also takes part in the crucial artistic decisions.

Richard Barr feels that a producer's involvement in artistic decisions should be kept to a minimum. "Choose the right people and let them go to work," Barr declares. "Then you keep your perspective, you function as a critic, which is exactly what you should be doing. Too many producers get their fingers in all the pies and they shouldn't be there at all, that's not their job. That's why you have a director, a costume designer, etc., etc. Obviously," Barr adds, "you can have the final say because you're presumably the boss. But we rarely exercise a veto unless there's a difference of opinion."

Choosing the play and "the right people" to put it together is the aspect of producing that Barr enjoys most. He is particularly enthusiastic about his discovery of Edward Albee. "I've had such an exciting time with him. I've fallen in love with every one of his plays as they've come along, and I don't feel there's one I preferred."

Though Edward Albee advised Mary Mercier on the script, it was decided that he would not be co-producer of *Johnny No-Trump,* but rather, the name of Charles Woodward, Jr. would appear on the marquee alongside those of Clinton Wilder and Richard Barr. So several months later, I arranged to meet Mr. Woodward. He is a stocky man with a crewcut and warm brown eyes, who said of himself, "I have backed plays for over twenty years and raised money for them, so I've been very close to producing for a long time." Charles Woodward had put money into all of Edward Albee's plays on Broadway except the least successful one, *Malcolm,* which ran less than a week. "In that case," Woodward said, "it happened to be borne out that I was correct, but many times I've done the same thing and I've been wrong."

Unlike Richard Barr, who spoke of finances reluctantly and called fund-raising "the onerous part of producing," Charles Woodward seemed to relish our discussion of "gambling" on Broadway. "You have to find people who are willing to gamble," he said, "because the theater is almost like the race track. And you can have a lot of fun if you don't put money into it that you can't afford to lose. Also, it takes longer to lose your money in the theater than it does in a horse race."

A play such as *Johnny No-Trump,* Woodward felt, was a better bet than a musical, "if you're only interested in making money. Because a musical may cost $500,000 and you have to play capacity audiences for forty weeks to break even. A musical must run years to make a lot of money, and you can have a musical that runs a year or two and doesn't return anything to the backers. A $5,000 investment in a $500,000 show is not the same thing as a $5,000 investment in a $100,000 show.

"If you get a hit in a straight play—*Mary, Mary* or *You Know I Can't Hear You When the Water's Running,* and hopefully *Johnny No-Trump*—you can make a great deal of money because the costs aren't so high. On the other hand, if we get bad notices with *Johnny No-Trump* we're through, maybe not that night but in a day or two. Musicals might be better in this way because they're not as subject to sudden closing. But believe me, if you were investing and really gambling, *Johnny No-Trump* would be a better bet than most musicals."

Chapter **4** **Casting the Play**

In the spring of 1967, shortly after a musical called *You're a Good Man, Charlie Brown* opened off-Broadway, *Johnny No-Trump* acquired a director. *Charlie Brown,* based on the Peanuts comic strip, was a resounding hit, and much of the credit went to its director, Joseph Hardy. *New York Times* drama critic Walter Kerr wrote that Joseph Hardy "seems to have flown *You're a Good Man, Charlie Brown* into place as gently as a kite on a nice day."

Joseph Hardy knew Mary Mercier, and in fact had read *Johnny No-Trump* in 1965, but it was the successful production of *Charlie Brown* that resulted in an offer from Richard Barr to direct *Johnny No-Trump.* This would be Hardy's first chance to direct on Broadway.

As director, Joe Hardy was responsible for casting the play along with the producer and the playwright. Some of the roles were cast by audition, but the majority were simply offered to actors and actresses whose work was familiar to either Joe Hardy or Richard Barr. Joe had come to know many actors during his six years directing television soap operas; others he met through work in live theater at Barnard College, Lincoln Center, and off-Broadway. As for Richard Barr, he is said to keep a "magic list" of actors he has seen and liked. Barr is a frequent and far-ranging theatergoer, and his list includes many little-known actors. "Richard Barr even goes off-off-Broadway," observed actress Barbara Lester. "After all these years he's still stagestruck."

Barbara Lester was, in fact, one of those whom Barr remembered, and he and Joe Hardy cast her in the small role of Mrs. Franklin in *Johnny No-Trump*. She was the only member of the cast who had worked for Barr previously, when she understudied in Edward Albee's *A Delicate Balance*. In *Johnny No-Trump* she would also understudy Florence and Nanna.

An actress who had played on Broadway only once before, and then very briefly, was picked for Florence. She was Sada Thompson, and had appeared in the musical *Maggie*, which ran for sixteen nights in the spring of 1959. "It only lasted about a minute," was the way Sada remembered it.

Sada Thompson was mailed a copy of the script of *Johnny No-Trump* in the spring of 1967. Her response was, "I liked the part, but then I liked the play mainly, and I liked Mary's wonderful ear for character—particularly the uncle. I laughed till I cried at that first scene. But then as I read, I came to feel that they were all quite distinctive, and I thought there were nice things to be worked on in this role."

Though she had appeared only once on Broadway, Sada Thompson was an actress of impressive experience. She had done plays of nearly every period, including Shakespeare, Chekhov, Molière, O'Neill, Tennessee Williams, and an adaptation of John Dos Passos's novel *U.S.A.* But her experience had been most of all classical, which made Sada feel that producers tended to think of her as unsuited to modern plays. "Except," she said, "when you find a producer with imagination." Richard Barr was such a producer, and "had seen practically everything I'd done without my knowing it."

Perhaps the most crucial role to be cast in *Johnny No-Trump* was the part of Uncle Harry. At one time, Richard Barr, Joe Hardy and Mary Mercier considered Burgess Meredith for the role, but the actor who was ultimately cast as Harry was Pat Hingle, who had played on Broadway in 1955 in Tennessee Williams's *Cat on a Hot Tin Roof*, starred in William Inge's *Dark at the Top of the Stairs,* and played the title role in Archibald MacLeish's *J.B.*

Perhaps because of his own years of hard times, Pat Hingle felt an immediate empathy with Harry in *Johnny No-Trump.* "Because I'm very practical by nature, much more so than a lot of actors I know, I really feel close to that aspect of Harry. I remember the Depression very vividly. And though Harry is a little more hepped on the price of things than I am, I worry about things like keeping the roof shingled and the rent paid.

"I took the role of Harry," he added, "because this was the best play that came to me. I came into it feeling there was a play under all this verbiage. This play was terribly verbose. There were four recognizable characters, but all of them talked so bloody much that all four just got to be bloody boring and alike in that they all talked so much. Possibly if it had been a lean year I might not have done it, because this was not a sure-fire play. But I'd just had a very lucrative three months making a movie in California. I knew that unless they found a Johnny— forget it. So when Barr called me at the beginning of the summer, I said 'Have you got a Johnny?' and he said, 'We've got two. We're just trying to decide between them.' Well, I'd never worked for Barr and I didn't know Joe Hardy, but I knew that Barr had just too good a track record not to hire good people, so I decided to do the show."

The role of Johnny's father, Alec, was also cast without an audition. The producer, director, and playwright all agreed on James Broderick, who had appeared on Broadway in Eugene O'Neill's *A Touch of the Poet,* in several off-Broadway plays, in the movie *The Group,* and on television in everything from soap operas to *The Iceman Cometh.*

James Broderick received a copy of the script of *Johnny No-Trump* while playing in Murray Shisgal's *Luv* in Santa Fe, New Mexico. He was debating whether to take the role, when the script was followed up by a telegram from Richard Barr, inviting him to "come join Sada Thompson and Pat Hingle in *Johnny No-Trump.*"

"I thought that seemed like a pretty good cast," Broderick said, "so I decided to do it." He accepted in August, only a few weeks before rehearsals were to begin.

The role of Johnny was cast by audition. Richard Barr remembered a tall, red-headed nineteen-year-old named Don Scardino who had auditioned for him for Edward Albee's *Malcolm,* also a play about a young boy, and he sent Don the script in March 1966. Don recalled thinking then, "I'd give my eyeteeth to play this part, but I'm probably too tall and too old. After all, the script says he's a short, funny-looking kid."

Soon afterward, an audition for potential Johnnys was held on the set of Edward Albee's *A Delicate Balance.* Don remembers reading for the part: "Richard Barr and Mary Mercier were in the house, and I read the opening scene with the uncle. The stage manager was reading the uncle's part in a monotone. I decided to move around the stage some during the reading—sometimes I'd rather move in auditions, sometimes not. I thought afterward that it was good but not great. But Mary Mercier came backstage and shook my hand, told me I'd done a nice job."

When Don learned that the production of *Johnny No-Trump* was being postponed until fall 1967, he was sure that by then he would be considered too old for the part. But several months later, he heard through the grapevine that it was still between two boys, himself and Richard Thomas, a sixteen-year-old he had once understudied. In July 1967 he was asked to read again.

"There were about twelve kids there, and they were all shorter and younger than I was. I read three pages of the first scene, and thought I was very dull. A week later, they called to tell me that I had the part. All of a sudden I started having qualms about doing such a big part. (Johnny would be Don's first major role on Broadway, although he had done small parts before.) I got cold feet and didn't want to take it. My agency thought I was crazy. They said it was such a fantastic opportunity, I had to accept it."

Aside from Johnny, the only other role cast by audition was Bettina. Even before Joe Hardy was hired as director, nineteen-year-old Bernadette Peters had been sent by her agent to read the part of Bettina for Richard Barr and Mary Mercier. "They laughed a lot, so I guess they liked me," was Bernadette's impression. Later, by a happy coincidence, Bernadette also auditioned for a replacement role in *You're a Good Man, Charlie Brown*. There Joe Hardy saw and liked her, and suggested to Barr that she would be right for Bettina. Barr had liked her at the earlier audition, and after a second reading Bernadette was given the part.

Although they were both only nineteen, Don Scardino and Bernadette Peters brought years of experience to their roles in *Johnny No-Trump*. Bernadette had first acted professionally at the age of nine. "I sang and I tap-danced," she says, "and I had a very low voice, which was pretty funny coming out of a kid. I didn't work much, though, because I wasn't a commercial-type child. I used to rebel at auditions. I'd see these kids sitting there, smiling great big phony grins, and I'd refuse to do it and just stand there like a dud."

As for Don, at thirteen he had begun "making the rounds" with his portfolio of photographs. "Making the rounds" can mean just about anything an actor has nerve enough to do. Don called at producers' offices to inquire about productions in the offing, or simply left his photographs and résumé for consideration. He also attended "open calls" where each actor who comes is interviewed briefly about his past work, and then may be asked to come back later and read for the part being cast. The actors' union, Equity, requires these of all Broadway and off-Broadway producers when they are casting. Usually a stage manager or production assistant conducts the interviews, but sometimes the director, playwright, or producer attends. Open calls supposedly give beginners a break, but most actors looking for work regard them cynically. An actor writing in the *New York Times* analyzed the logic behind open calls this way: "All the actors in New York (of whom there are roughly fifteen thousand) who somehow learn that a three-character play is casting must be given a day or two during which they can be turned down en masse."

In general, there is a baffling rule that young actors and actresses like Don and Bernadette confront everywhere—if you want to do something, you have to have done something already. This applies especially to the first practical requirement for getting a part in any Broadway show, and most off-Broadway shows: to be hired you must belong to the actor's union, Equity, but in order to belong to Equity, you must already have played in an Equity production.

Circular as it sounds, there *are* ways of getting into Equity. Don Scardino had managed to get his Equity card by answering an ad in *Show Business,* a trade newspaper that publishes job information. (*Backstage, Variety,* and the bulletin board at the midtown office of Actor's Equity are also helpful.) The ad announced that the summer stock production of *Critic's Choice* was casting. Even a chorus role in an Equity stock production entitles an actor to a union card. So when Don went to the audition, and got the role, he also got his Equity membership, and "from then on I just sort of kept working." Don adds, "There's a certain thing about momentum. All you have to do is get in something good and get your name around. Then the jobs seems to follow."

Membership in Equity at the time *Johnny No-Trump* was produced, guaranteed Don a minimum wage of not less than $70.00 a week off-Broadway, and $137.50 a week on Broadway. This is in return for payment of annual dues of thirty dollars, for those earning less than $2,500 a year. Dues rise up to two hundred dollars for those with annual salaries of $20,000 or more. Significantly, however, of 14,000 members in Equity, the great majority (about eighty-five percent) earned less than $5,000 in 1967, and fewer than eighty actors and actresses earned more than $25,000 from work on the stage.

Don Scardino also credits his success to a very large agency, called General Artists Corporation. He signed with them at sixteen, and says that he has never been out of work since. There are a number of different kinds of agencies in New York which may be helpful to actors. Casting agencies keep voluminous files of actors' résumés and photographs. Through their contacts, they occasionally come up with parts for their clients, although they are usually bit parts in movies and television.

For meatier roles, there are individual theatrical agents to whom Broadway producers send announcements of their casting requirements and descriptions of the roles available. The agents, in turn, submit the names of their actor-clients, and if one of them gets a part, the agent will receive ten percent of his salary.

Unfortunately, however, most agents are not likely to be interested in novices who merely knock at their doors. They ask for tangible proof of ability and experience, and usually want to see an actor perform. Also, by Equity regulation, the agents are not entitled to receive the ten percent commission unless their client's salary is at least a Broadway minimum of $137.50, and so they are not likely to go out of their way to find off-Broadway roles. Thus, for beginners, these individual agents also focus largely on television and movies.

Some agents specialize in movies or television, some in musical comedy. There are one-man agencies with posh East-side offices, but one actor I met described a one-woman agency like this: "She was quite an elderly lady with a very disorganized office on Times Square. I see her in a housedress and gym shoes—I don't know, perhaps she wasn't wearing them, but that's the kind of lady she was. She had one fellow working for her there, but he looked like a volunteer. And she had this pay phone in her office, which she did all her telephoning on." Despite the fly-by-night look of the place, however, this agent got the actor an interview for a major movie.

It was forty-three-year-old Pat Hingle, cast as Uncle Harry in *Johnny No-Trump,* who conveyed to me the most vivid impressions of what it means to try to make sense out of the maze of agents and producers' offices. Now a successful actor, Pat no longer has to "make the rounds." But in 1949, when he arrived in New York City with a young wife, a degree in radio from the University of Texas, and no acquaintances in the professional theater, things were quite different. He had enrolled in drama classes at a school called the American Theater Wing, and he reminisces, "I would just kind of half go to auditions. I'd find a couple of places advertised in *Show Business,* and my morality would say I should try to get a job, so I'd show up and then leave. I had this shnook agent at the time. Every time I'd come into his office, he'd look at me and say, 'I never have a call for your type.' " Hingle gave a wide-eyed look.

Eventually, he told me, "I decided making rounds has got to be a thing that has nothing to do with talent. It can't be talent since they just look at you and say no most of the time. It must be largely luck. So I figured the best way to approach it would be through sheer volume of coverage. I decided to plan a campaign."

He did just that. He hung brown wrapping paper the full length of one wall of his apartment, and on it charted a huge calendar, with an empty square for each day of the coming five months. "If I read in the newspaper that Kermit Bloomgarten was casting a play in the early spring, I'd go to my calendar. In March somewhere I'd put, 'See Kermit Bloomgarten.' "

Another strategy was a little book in which he wrote down the names of contacts he made. "When I'd go to a producer's office, there'd always be some little girl at the front desk acting like she was God Almighty. I'd ask her if there was any casting going on that day, and she'd say, 'No casting today.' And I'd ask if she knew what day the producer might be casting the show. And she'd say, 'No day.' " But Pat would persist until he had some idea of when he might come back. Then, before leaving, he would say, "You know my name but I don't know yours." The girl would look surprised, "because nobody usually asks these girls their names, and she'd tell me. As soon as I got out the door, her name would go down in my little book. The next time I called, I would call the girl by name and already I'd be one up."

Finally, "through sheer volume of coverage," Hingle began to get parts. Small parts. "I played so many cop extras on TV that they had a special cop outfit at Brooks Costume laid aside for me. All the TV people had to do was call down and say, 'Get out Pat Hingle's costume.' They just changed the insignia according to what kind of cop I was playing that day. I usually came on at the end. There'd be someone saying, 'Take this guy away,' and I'd grab the heavy and drag him off. I had no lines."

But there were compensations. "You can live on that income. And there is the satisfaction, when you fill out your meager little tax form, that you don't put down waiter or something else, you put down actor."

Rehearsals for *Johnny No-Trump* began on September 5, 1967. All the parts had been cast except for one—the role of Nanna. Suggestions came from everyone (even I suggested an actress and was taken seriously), but it was Mary Mercier who finally cast Anne Ives.

Mary had seen and liked the work of this elderly actress in an out-of-town production of *All the Way Home*. All she could remember about her, however, was that she lived at the Dakota, an elegant old apartment house where many theater people live. With the Dakota as a clue, Anne Ives was tracked down and asked to read for the part. By the fourth day of rehearsals, *Johnny No-Trump* had a Nanna.

Chapter 5 At the Cort Theater

On the morning of September 7, 1967, the Broadway theater district from Forty-second Street to Fiftieth Street was still in its summer doldrums. The marquees advertised the previous season's hits or nothing at all. At the Cort Theater on Forty-eighth Street between Sixth and Seventh Avenues, the marquee was blank, and the glass display cases out front were empty. Alongside the Cort was an alleyway closed off from the street by an iron fence. This morning the fence gate was slightly ajar.

I walked into the alleyway, which was dark even in the bright summer morning. The only light came from two bare bulbs, one on the side wall and the other over what I presumed was the stage door, at the top of a dozen iron steps. Just inside, an elderly doorman in a 1940s-style suit sat in a cubbyhole, reading a newspaper and drinking coffee from a plastic cup. I explained to him that I had come to watch the rehearsals of *Johnny No-Trump*. He directed me to walk straight ahead into the wings.

It was not quite ten-thirty, the time when rehearsal was scheduled to begin. The stage manager, Don Kohler, and his assistant, Charles Kindl, were already at work at a card table offstage, thumbing through a looseleaf copy of the script and drawing up a list of props. The Cort stage itself was awesomely bare. There were no vestiges of the play that had previously occupied that space, and only a few pieces of furniture that would be used during the rehearsals of *Johnny No-Trump.*

Scores of plays have appeared at the Cort Theater since December 20, 1912, when the first audience filed into the red plush orchestra seats and two baroque balconies, delicately ornamented in white and gold. That night, Laurette Taylor opened the theater in *Peg O' My Heart,* one of the most popular plays of the decade, which ran at the Cort for 605 performances. Laurence Olivier and Judith Anderson have performed at the Cort, and Katherine Hepburn made her New York debut here. Yet as I watched the actors enter one by one to begin rehearsing *Johnny No-Trump,* it seemed to me that it would take a miracle to fill the huge and empty Cort stage with a play.

The first of the cast to arrive was Don Scardino, the tall, slender nineteen-year-old who would play the title role of Johnny. Don was wearing dungarees and a plaid shirt, and his thick red hair was well below his ears. He sat down on a stool at center stage to wait for the others, and began making tentative sounds on a harmonica.

Around him was the worn furniture the cast would make do with during early rehearsals, before the actual set arrived. In the "living room," at stage right (from the point of view of an actor facing the audience), was a stuffed armchair for Uncle Harry. Opposite it was a wooden bench with a slatted back, fast shedding its gray paint. Eventually, that bench would be a sofa. Upstage (that is, at the back of the stage; downstage is at the front) and slightly to the right was a small table representing a desk, with a telephone and binoculars on it. The dining area was at stage left, dominated by a makeshift table with a loose top and two soda-fountain chairs. Otherwise, the props were mostly cleaning things for Mrs. Franklin: a can of Ajax, several aerosols, a burlap bag full of cloth scraps to represent laundry, and a mop and broom. Bright yellow tape had been laid out on the floor of the stage, defining the perimeters of the set, and doors and stairs. The tape pattern was most complicated up center (a stage direction meaning centered at the back), where it defined each step of an imaginary staircase, climbed halfway up to an imaginary landing, then turned.

As I was looking around, Pat Hingle walked onstage and began to talk with Don Scardino. Hingle is a man of stocky build, six feet tall and vigorous-looking despite a slight limp. He wore a sportshirt outside his cotton pants, and moccasins. He took the harmonica from Don and began to play a tune in chords.

"How do you do that?" Don asked. "Are you covering up something with that other hand?" Don turned his face up to Hingle, his deep-set eyes peering at Hingle's bushy eyebrows. He took the harmonica back and said, "Now I'm going to play like Dylan." It seemed unlikely, and Pat Hingle grinned, transforming his changeable face and causing deep wrinkles to appear around his blue eyes.

Meanwhile, Barbara Lester, the actress who would play Mrs. Franklin, arrived and sat down on a cot in the wings to study her script. Director Joe Hardy was at stage right, talking to the stage managers. Hardy is a short, balding man with large eyes and a square jaw. He was also dressed informally, in khaki pants and a blue workshirt. He hadn't noticed Barbara Lester, and asked the stage manager if she had arrived. Then, checking the time on his mod watch (the only thing he wore that was at all theatrical), he said, "I think we're ready to begin."

A stepladder had been set up temporarily to connect the stage to the orchestra below, and I used it to step down into the house. Later in rehearsals, director Joe Hardy would also watch from the house, but today he chose to hover onstage close to Pat Hingle and Don Scardino as they ran through the opening lines of scene one. They worked at first without scripts, taking an occasional cue from Charles Kindl, who was "holding book" as prompter at stage left. It wasn't long, however, before Pat Hingle said, "Well, that's as far as I go," and pushed himself up from Uncle Harry's chair to go get his script.

Today, Thursday, was actually the third day of rehearsals. There had been a sit-down reading on Tuesday, and the actors had gotten on their feet for the first time on Wednesday. Don and Pat were learning their lines quickly. Pat seemed already to be building a characterization.

He had captured a sense of the older, tired man he was playing (Hingle is forty-three and the character of Harry is in his sixties), and had done it so quickly that my impression of Pat was from the first modified by the impression he gave of Harry.

Pat Hingle and Don Scardino were also beginning to build the rapport so essential to a successful interpretation of the play. At one point in the scene, Hingle, script in hand, walked over to Don and affectionately mussed his hair. The stage suddenly seemed full.

This morning Joe Hardy concentrated on Johnny's first entrance, when he intentionally gets under Harry's skin. Hardy wanted Don to be more active. "The kid can't sit still," he told him. "After all, he's sixteen and an adolescent, and God knows what changes are going on in his body. He's full of excess energy he has to use up."

Inventing detail, or "business" for Johnny became the joint effort of the director and actors. Sometimes Don Scardino had an idea, and Joe Hardy saw it through to its logical conclusion. For instance, as Johnny reaches the bottom of the stairs, the script calls for him to pick up a pair of binoculars and peer at Harry. At first Don tried looking at Hingle from a distance, then he tried examining the rug for a minute, at very close range. So Hardy suggested, "Walk up and examine *Harry* at close range." In the next run-through, Don brought the binoculars within inches of his "uncle's" face. Pat Hingle, who hadn't known in advance that Don would do this, immediately growled, as Harry would have done, and pushed the binoculars aside.

Another example: Johnny is supposed to look for a missing tennis shoe. Hardy told Don to "really look for it" under the couch, and this time Pat Hingle came up with an embellishment. "Why not have the shoe under Uncle Harry's chair?" Hardy agreed, "All right, have fun with it, that's the main thing." Now Uncle Harry, already rankled by his nephew, will have the further annoyance of Johnny burrowing under his feet.

Such invention would later prove Don Scardino's forte, but today he seemed too inhibited to "have fun with it." He was very much awed by having a lead in a Broadway play, and particularly playing opposite Pat

Hingle, a Broadway veteran. Pat must have sensed this, for during one break he walked up to Don and said, "Don't hesitate to try anything you want to. I'll go along. What I do depends to a great extent on what you do." He made a similar gesture to the assistant stage manager and prompter, Chuck Kindl. "Sometimes I forget a line and I'll yell for it," he told him. "If I sound angry it's not that I'm angry at you, I'm angry at myself for forgetting it."

After the rehearsal break, Sada Thompson appeared briefly onstage as Johnny's schoolteacher-mother, Florence. Sada, who has a sixteen-year-old daughter of her own, is a woman in her thirties, feminine and slightly plump. Her full-skirted print dress was a little long, there were touches of gray in her short brown hair, and she wore eyeglasses. She looked, in fact, like a schoolteacher.

Shortly after her entrance, Joe Hardy called a lunch break. Only he and Don Scardino remained onstage to work on scene one; I stood in the wings, intending to watch them.

Instead, I found myself looking at Sada Thompson, who was eating a sandwich at a small table in the wings. What intrigued me about her was a quality I had seen before in accomplished actresses: each movement as she ate, reading *Show Business* at the same time, was clear, separate, and purposeful. Later, Sada handled props on stage with equal deliberateness. Once when I asked her about this, she corrected me. "I think you mean objects, not props. After all, they should be objects, not props, if you're working well."

The handling of objects, real and imaginary, became the focal point of the afternoon rehearsal. Joe Hardy concentrated on scene two, when Florence and Harry argue over Johnny's future. The argument takes place over lunch, and to my surprise, Hardy focused more on the lunch than the argument.

The script merely indicates that Florence puts out a sandwich for Harry and one for herself. The director and actors took it from there. They imagined, first, that both sandwiches were uncut, so Hardy suggested that Florence cut her own and then reach across the table with a knife to cut Harry's. Hardy also thought Harry would want mustard, but would Florence be likely to pass him the mustard, or would he have to go out to the kitchen to get it? The script says Harry is a great coffee drinker, so he probably wants coffee, too. No doubt he will get up and go to the kitchen for the pot made that morning. But Harry is practical. He wouldn't put a coffeepot down on the wooden dining table without a hotpad. There was a brief search for a hotpad, and when the stage manager came up with an old square block of wood, Hingle, always agreeable, dubbed it "marvelous."

Next came the matter of cups and saucers. Harry would, of course, bring a cup and saucer for himself, but would he bring them for his sister, too? Yes, he should bring two, and pour coffee for them both.

Now that the coffee was poured, what about cream and sugar? Did Harry take either or both? And Florence? Pat Hingle had an insight. "I know what Harry uses. Harry uses saccharin. Harry has to go get his little bottle of saccharin for his coffee. And if he's like me, he uses one and a half tablets, because one isn't enough. So what you do is, you put one in, then you take another one, and you take a knife, and you split that mother in half and put half in."

Everyone laughed, but from then on, whenever Harry had a cup of coffee, he or whoever brought it to him also brought a saccharin bottle and a knife, put in one tablet, and then cut a second one in half.

Joe Hardy seemed delighted with the day's progress. Unlike him, I went away from rehearsal slightly disappointed. I had expected these professionals to be precise, and I had found them so. Indeed, no detail seemed too slight for their consideration. But this, after all, was only the third day of rehearsal. Couldn't Harry's saccharin tablets have waited until the actors worked out the emotional dynamics of the scene? Obviously, the director did not think so.

Chapter **6** The Director

I suppose what I had been expecting from director Joseph Hardy was the kind of analysis that can be found in the writings of director Elia Kazan. In the notebooks he kept while directing Tennessee Williams's *A Streetcar Named Desire,* Kazan jotted down a short phrase about each major character, describing the heart of the role, what he called the "spine" of the character. Then he wrote a brilliant, rather lengthy study of each.

But after a week of rehearsals, I stopped expecting Joe Hardy to analyze either the characters in *Johnny No-Trump* or the play itself. It was simply not his style. What impressed me, though, was that while his direction seemed to remain on the surface much of the time, the actors' performances did not. As I saw the excellent results he was getting, my respect for his direction increased.

I had been surprised by his immediate attention to "coffee and saccharin," but Sada Thompson later told me, "There were things that I found hard in that scene (the lunch scene) with Harry. I loved the writing there, but I found, at least in the rudimentary stages of rehearsal, that I was apt to take too literally what seemed the relationship there between Harry and Florence. That whole scene became too belligerent, and didn't reflect the sort of years of being together between Florence and Harry."

In light of this, Hardy's approach to the scene began to make more sense. Florence cutting Harry's sandwich, Harry pouring Florence's coffee—these things mitigated the harsh words the brother and sister were exchanging, and helped to convey the feeling that they had lived together for years. Comments like Sada's suggested to me that Joe Hardy often got at the real problems of a scene indirectly.

Despite this, and despite the fact that the director frequently had long conversations with the actors in their dressing rooms, it is probably fair to conclude, as James Broderick did, that "Joe Hardy is not a diggy-down kind of director." Many directors spend several days at the start of rehearsals reading and discussing the play with the actors, or improvising situations similar to those in the play. Others, like the British director-actor Sir Laurence Olivier, reject such analysis. "I'd rather have run a scene eight times," Olivier has said, "than have wasted time in chattering about abstractions. An actor gets the right thing by doing it over and over. Arguing about motivations and so forth is a lot of rot. American directors encourage that sort of thing too much . . . Instead of doing a scene over again that's giving them trouble, they want to discuss . . . discuss . . . discuss."

In the view of another British director, Sir Tyrone Guthrie, a director's most creative function is to listen, "to be at rehearsal a highly receptive, highly concentrated, highly critical sounding board for the performance, an audience of one. He (the director) is not the drill sergeant, not the schoolmaster, and he does not sweep in with a lot of verbiage and 'Stand here and do it this way, darling, and move the right hand, not the left.' He is simply receiving the thing, transmitting it and giving it back."

To be "an audience of one" at rehearsals is important, but rehearsals themselves are only one among many concerns of the director. He coordinates all aspects of a production, linking actors and playwright, and often knows better than a playwright what will work and what won't. The director's concept of a play influences the design of sets, lighting, and costumes, and in fact nearly everything. The least specialized member of the company, he sees to it that all the efforts of the specialists—actors, designer, playwright—come together to realize a work of art.

To do this well obviously requires the broadest possible grounding in theater. Yevgeny Vakhtangov, a distinguished Russian director, believed so thoroughly in the need to educate young directors diversely that he started off his students hanging up coats in the cloakroom of his Mansurov Studio in Moscow. If they objected, he told them, "No director . . . whose task is to serve the spectator should be afraid of soiling his hands touching other people's galoshes." From the cloakroom, Vakhtangov's students graduated to being stagehands, then on to doing lights, costumes, and props. Only after two years backstage did they begin working with actors.

Vakhtangov's students had an ideal school in which to learn their craft: a permanent theater. In the United States, however, there has not been, until recently, sufficient public enthusiasm for theater to support permanent companies. As a result, the education of American directors is frequently a patchwork affair.

Joe Hardy's certainly has been—first in the far west, then in Paris, and finally in New York. "Put this in your book," Joe told me one day after rehearsal. "Theater has never been considered a really legitimate profession in this country. Because of our puritanical background, the theater as a whole was thought bad, evil in some way. As a result, there is nowhere in this country where you can train early enough. In England you can decide you want to be an actor or director and go off to Diddly-Poo-on-the-Sea, and there'll be a repertory company there where you can be trained. But not in this country."

Relaxing over a drink, Joe remarked that his career as a director had been rather improbable—he grew up on a ranch in Las Vegas, learning "to rope, brand a calf." But as early as high school, Joe began going to see all the theater he could. He attended the University of Las Vegas to study drama and, following a brief, ill-starred plan to make it on his own after his freshman year, from then on "never really stopped."

At the university, he directed ten plays, completed a master's degree in French, and became convinced he was going to be a director. "Acting, after all, is limited," he said. "You can only make one character come to life. I wanted to make all the characters come to life."

After a year in Paris on a Fulbright scholarship, during which Joe went to the French theater about five times a week, and another M.A., in theater, from Yale University, Joe came to New York City with ten dollars in his pocket and a determination to make his way as a professional director.

He began in television soap operas, and in seven years rose from script editor to producer. He doesn't regret his soap-opera years because, "when you work with that kind of live material, a half-hour script a day, two and a half hours of live material a week, you learn how to work with writers on an intense level."

The turning point in his career had been the off-Broadway play *You're a Good Man, Charlie Brown.* And now, of course, there was *Johnny No-Trump.* Considering it was his first Broadway production, Joe was remaining remarkably cool. "It's coming along beautifully," he told me one day early in rehearsals as he perused Broadway through a pair of wrap-around sunglasses. "The only thing I'm worried about now is that it will be over-rehearsed."

Joe came to rehearsals with no notes and no set ideas on staging. "When I was younger I used to stage things," he said. "I don't do that any more." I asked him what *Johnny No-Trump* was about, and he said simply that it was "a play about love."

He did, however, have a concept of the play. "You must come to rehearsals with a concept," he told me. "Always. My concept of *Johnny No-Trump* was that it would be as realistic as possible within the framework of extended characters. They aren't really real people, you know. They're all written, because Mary writes like that, just a little larger than life. It isn't like playing Chekhov, or Odets even, because they're a little bigger than that. Given that concept, you then cast people like Sada and Jimmy and Don and Pat, because they play bigger than most people play."

After *Johnny No-Trump* was cast, he concentrated on building a rapport with the actors. "Actors are more vulnerable than anybody," he said. "If they weren't, they wouldn't be good actors. In order to be a good actor, you have to be immature in some way, in order to immerse yourself totally in a role. When you're up there onstage, you have to reveal yourself completely. I can't do it, I don't understand how they can, but thank heavens there are people who can. It's important to the director to be very cognizant of human beings. You'd better understand the actors well, and you'd better understand them during the first three days of rehearsals, because you can make mistakes then that will be disastrous later on."

Joe was supportive of the actors during rehearsals. Most of his comments were prefaced by a kind word—"Much better," or "It's coming along beautifully." With Pat Hingle, he was respectful but not uncritical. He was more informal with Don Scardino, often putting his arm around him as he spoke. "Joe Hardy had a sense of humor," Don once said to me, "and I appreciated that. He used to walk by me sometimes during rehearsals and say, 'Boy, that was some play-acting!'"

Like Joe, Don had worked on daytime television (in a soap opera called *The Guiding Light,* which Don called "the Guiding Plight"), but he found the live stage very different. "One of the pitfalls of working on the soaps," Don explained, "is that you have to learn the script quickly— they give it to you the day before. So you're always racing ahead to think of the next line, and you don't listen to the other actors. Joe used to tell me all the time, 'Think and listen.' He'd say to me, 'Ideas—the ideas come before the words.' Sometimes he'd pass by my dressing room saying, 'Ideas, ideas, ideas.'"

Joe liked to work quickly, but he also accepted the actors' need to work at their own pace. There were times when he concentrated on perfecting minute details from the outset, but many other times he let the actors experiment freely until something seemed to work, then "set" it. Don Scardino's first entrance, for instance, was done dozens of different ways before it was set. In one variation, Don struggled down the staircase like Frankenstein, while in another, he simply tapped his fingers on the bannister as he entered. "The actors had to feel free," Don said. "Sometimes Joe would say to me, 'Just let yourself fly, we'll bring it back later on.' "

Don had just acted under an English director, John Dexter, in a play called *The Unknown Soldier and His Wife*. He found Joe Hardy's approach to directing quite different, explaining that "the English tend to go more by the rules anyway. John Dexter was boss, law, God, and it was A B C D, do this and this and this. Then later, if something didn't go well, he'd sometimes make changes, but he had a definite idea of how he wanted everything staged. Whereas with Joe everything is flexible."

One of the first things Joe Hardy told me when he learned that I was writing a book about *Johnny No-Trump* was that the rehearsals would be calm, perhaps too calm to make an exciting story. The rehearsals, largely due to the way Joe worked, were indeed free of temperamental scenes. Only once did I see Joe angry. Mary Mercier had asked him rather sharply, during a break, why a section had been cut from the first act. Joe brushed off her question, but later came down to her in the house and said, quietly angry, "Don't ever do that in front of the actors. It upsets them."

It is significant that this flare-up concerned a cut in the play, for it was in the area of revisions that the most serious conflict occurred.

Chapter 7 Revisions

Richard Barr's approach to producing is based on a conviction that the script of a play should be in nearly finished form before rehearsals begin. "On Broadway," he once said in an interview in *Theater Arts* magazine, "it is such a hassle getting a theater and a star and a play all ready at the same time, that you are frequently forced into rehearsal before you're ready—before the play is ready, that is. That's the first thing we've learned . . . we are not going into rehearsal until the script we plan to open with on Broadway is in our hands. There will be changes made in that script, of course, but they'll be minor changes, not the terrible, frightening business of trying to create a whole new second or third act between New Haven and New York.

"Which brings us right up to the second point. If you start out with a finished play, there is no need for the (tryout) week in Wilmington or wherever, and two weeks in Philadelphia or Boston, where you're bound to lose a substantial amount of money. Three weeks of rehearsals and a week of paid previews are all you should need, if you've cast it right."

In July 1967, Richard Barr suggested the first major revision in the script of *Johnny No-Trump:* the elimination of a tomboy friend of Johnny's named Lucy. In the original script, Lucy came onstage toward the end of act two to announce the death of Johnny's mother. Barr suggested, instead, that Bettina, the sophisticated fifteen-year-old from next door, announce the death. Bettina, who in the original had only one scene, would thus be given two. "This way you'll get two sides of the same girl," Barr said, "which will be more interesting. You'll see her in that very funny first scene, and then a second time when she has to face a very serious moment." He added, "I don't think there will be many changes outside of that one."

But in August, and even during rehearsals in September, quite a few more changes were made after all. Joe Hardy and Mary Mercier first discussed cutting the play in August. According to Joe, he and Mary "went through the play and I marked all the cuts in my book. And I went down that evening to Dick Barr's. I showed him the cuts, and he said, 'Marvelous.' He called Clinton Wilder and told Clinton, 'This, this, and this is going.' Clinton said, 'This is great.' A week later, we were like three days from rehearsal and Mary had not done a thing about the cuts, so I finally had to do it myself. Fortunately, I had the cuts marked."

Joe Hardy considers himself "one of the most lenient of directors" in his relationship with the playwright, "because I believe in the writer so strongly, and I believe that's where it is. But I do think ultimately that the director has to be the one who finally says, 'No, it won't work. It will work. No, I won't do that scene that way.' It's just like playwrights directing their own plays—they should never do it. They cannot be objective enough. They don't want to cut their precious, bloody words, and some of them need to be cut. Certainly there needs to be an objectivity about the approach that no writer, because it's such sweat to get it down on paper, can possibly have. So ultimately it has to be the director."

Whatever she had agreed to previously, Mary Mercier had expected to see her long version of act two onstage. When rehearsals began with the cuts in effect (ultimately act two was reduced by half), Mary was angry and dismayed. "There's so much of the second act they just refuse to stage," she said about ten days into rehearsals. "Hardy sat down with the script from the very beginning and started making cuts. You can't do that. You must see it on its feet before you can rewrite."

The difficulty arose in part from the necessity of having *Johnny No-Trump* nearly at performance level after only three weeks of rehearsal. Joseph Hardy was temperamentally suited for this, while Mary Mercier was not. Joe liked to work fast, to "get the play on its feet as quickly as possible," and he didn't "believe in over-rehearsing." Mary Mercier was less aware of deadlines. "She did not know the limitations of time," Joe said, "and she had a terrible problem about thinking we could just futz around with it for two or three weeks and see if it worked. Well, you can't do that. That's why you hire good directors—you hope— that's why you hope you have good producers who say, 'One, two, three' " —Hardy snapped his fingers—" 'Out, out, out, before we even begin to rehearse, we know this isn't going to work.' "

It is possible that *Johnny No-Trump* might have benefited from the extra time provided by out-of-town tryouts. Though Richard Barr argues against them, other producers defend tryouts because they give a writer more time to revise and a better atmosphere in which to do it.

One co-producer of five Broadway shows, and manager of many more, says, "Theoretically, I agree with Richard Barr. Ideally, a play should be in final form when rehearsals begin, but the fact is that plays often aren't. And if you have to make changes and revisions, the best place to do it is out-of-town. When you're out-of-town, there are no distractions. The actors don't have to worry about a sick baby at home, or doing the laundry. You're away from your friends—God save you from your friends! They come backstage after previews and tell you that you've got to get rid of the costume you wear in the second scene, and so on. The gossip about a play before it opens is ninety-nine percent destructive. But when you're out-of-town, you're away from all that. There's only the theater, the play, and the hotel."

Certainly *Johnny No-Trump* was not the ideal, finished play Barr preferred when the brief New York rehearsal period began. On the tenth day of rehearsals, the actors were shuffling the pages of a freshly typed revision.

Chapter **8** The Actors

Constantin Stanislavski, the Russian drama teacher and director whose theories on technique have had great influence on many actors, wrote in his book *An Actor Prepares* that creating a role, like creating a child, takes nine months. Broadway actors, however, must pace themselves over a much shorter period of time, usually a month. Sometimes a role grows gradually and steadily during this month; at other times, very little seems to be happening until a sudden breakthrough occurs.

None of the actors in *Johnny No-Trump* could single out a particular day or insight that brought their roles suddenly to life for them. Yet at one time or another, during rehearsals and after, when I asked the actors how they went about conceiving their roles, they were able to provide glimpses into their creative processes. Three actors—James Broderick who played Alec, Barbara Lester who played Mrs. Franklin, and Sada Thompson who played Florence—had especially interesting responses to my questions.

James Broderick/Alec. "When I come onstage as Alec," James Broderick began, "I have forty-one years of living behind me. Now that's something to consider."

Broderick is a tall, slender man of forty, just a year younger than the character he plays. He has round eyes, bushy brows, and a short nose —features that make him a natural for Irish plays. The movement of his hands suggests that he is a nervous person, but his face often bears an expression of amused detachment.

About creating the character of Alec he said, "Sometimes I have a good idea of what the character's all about before rehearsing. Other times I don't like to have too set an idea. But I really don't start moving in a part until I see the other actors and what they're like. I thought about *Johnny No-Trump* before rehearsals began, but I mostly thought about what Alec did outside the house. I thought about why he left the house, why he came to the birthday party, whether he's good with women, good in bed. I think I finally decided that he was good in bed, and I tried to show that, especially in the scenes with Bettina.

"Some things bother me, but when I start to play them, if they work I don't think about them any more. Like why Alec came to the birthday party. I think I decided that he came because he needed fifty dollars."

Broderick was more definite about why Alec left his wife and son. "He left the house because he couldn't stand to be depended upon, couldn't stand it." He winced as Alec might have at the thought. "He hates Harry, absolutely cannot stand Harry. He tells Harry he has his own one-man show coming up and all Harry says is, 'You'll screw it up.' When Harry tells him his cuffs are frayed, that kills him.

"Alec doesn't feel like playing games, and with Harry you have to. Alec knows when he asks for a drink that Harry won't give it to him the first time, but that if he keeps asking he'll finally get it. It's like an adolescent with his father. When the kid asks his father for the car, he knows if he asks him enough times he'll finally get it. But Alec doesn't feel like playing that game any more.

"Alec isn't a pioneer like the grandmother," Broderick went on. "He tells his son, 'Don't let the bastards get you down.' Well, they have gotten *him* down. And he doesn't especially like it when his son wants to become a poet, because he'd like to be the only artist in the family."

Broderick did not believe that Alec felt much even when his wife died. "He doesn't feel much of anything any more.

"I thought a lot about alcoholics," he continued. "Joe Hardy said to me, 'He's not really an alcoholic.' But I said to Joe, 'You can't play that. You can't *play* that.' I think the line Alec has, 'You drink because your feel disappears,' isn't quite right. When you have a key line like that, you mull it over and over. I think maybe the line should be, 'You drink because you feel too much.'

"It's hard to say, but if you're an artist like Alec, say you want to draw a hand. You have this image in your mind of how it will look, you know, set back in the picture a certain way—like Rembrandt. But when you come to put it on paper, you can't get it to come out the way it was in your mind. And so you go over to the bar and have a few drinks and you talk about it. You say, 'I'm doing this wonderful drawing of a hand, and the arm comes in this certain way and it's marvelous!' And you really believe that, because that's your *life,* you see."

In working on the role of Alec, James Broderick drew on a long-time fascination with the life of Van Gogh. "Do you realize how long Van Gogh sketched and drew before he started to paint? He'd sketch and sketch, and then he'd say, 'No, I'm not quite ready to paint yet.' I think you have to be able to draw before you can paint. I tried to draw once—it's very difficult. First I tried to draw a tree. And then I tried to draw a hand. I worked and I worked, and finally I managed to get something down on paper that looked like my own hand. But it was hard."

Finally, in creating Alec, Broderick said he "went to a place where artists hang out. What is it called—Max's Kansas City? I went there late a couple of times, just to see what kind of place Alec might go to. Alec might have been a pretty good entertainer in some of those places some nights. But that's about all."

Barbara Lester/Mrs. Franklin.   The role of Mrs. Franklin in *Johnny No-Trump* is a small one. Just after the curtain rises, Mrs. Franklin enters from next door to do the cleaning, and announces, "Well, I'm here." She has seven more lines, all spoken as she goes about her cleaning, annoying Harry and embarrassing Johnny.

It is a role one might expect Barbara Lester to take easily in stride, after more than twenty years in the theater, a master's degree in drama from Columbia University, and 108 roles in stock, on Broadway, and off-Broadway. But I learned one day in her dressing room that Barbara Lester agonized over the role of Mrs. Franklin as much as anyone else in *Johnny No-Trump* did over their larger roles.

"Now as for this play," Barbara began, closing the door to her dressing room, "Barr didn't read anybody for this role. He saw me eight years ago in something, so when *A Delicate Balance* came along, he called me and asked me to read for the understudy for Rosemary Murphy, and I read and got the job. Now Richard Barr is very loyal and uses the same actors over and over again. So when they wanted someone to understudy Sada Thompson and, for convenience, to play Mrs. Franklin at the same time, they hired me."

Barbara Lester, who is English-born, is a large-boned woman with a deep voice and blonde hair. In conversation and appearance she is without pretense. Her usual rehearsal costume was a simple shift dress and flat shoes, and she wore glasses over her large, pretty eyes.

"I'm not right for Mrs. Franklin at all," she said. "She's at least fifty-five and I'm only thirty-eight. She's supposed to be a New Yorker and I still have traces of an English accent. In a case like this, you have to do a characterization. So I decided to go on big and then calm it down later on—to start working from the outside in."

I had frequently heard actors speak of "working from the outside in," or its opposite, "working from the inside out," but had never clearly understood either phrase. Barbara explained and gave me examples. "When I was nineteen I played an eighty-year-old in stock. Well, what you do is, you speak with the old voice (Barbara did this: a tight, cracking voice) and you carry the cane—it's absolutely outside. It's sort of based on what you see other actors doing and what you see old people doing, but it's not from within yourself. I had no idea what an eighty-year-old person felt. There are many times in stock when I'll work from the outside in because everything is so rushed. You hope by opening night, but it's usually by Saturday, by the time you've had the reviews already, that you're getting more and more truthful.

"Now if you were going to do an old lady and you decided to work from the inside out, that is work from yourself, you would think, for instance, of how you feel when your back aches from painting the apartment and you can't sit down so easily. Then you eventually would sit down like an old lady might sit down. That's working from your own feeling of how your back hurts when you've strained it, as opposed to right away indicating that your back hurts though you're not feeling it. Either way is all right, so long as it results in success."

In creating the role of Mrs. Franklin, who first comes in out of the pouring rain, Barbara called on an incident that had occurred one evening when she and a friend were drenched in a sudden downpour. Barbara thought, "This is all I need for the entrance. If I can just remember this feeling of being drenched, it will help me."

But because she felt Mrs. Franklin was so different from herself, Barbara chose to work mainly from the outside in. After Joe Hardy commented that Mrs. Franklin probably annoys Harry, she tried a heavy walk in going about her chores in the Edwards' house. She worked to capture the quality of a woman of fifty-five or sixty. And she tried to replace her English accent with a New York accent.

The accent, according to Barbara, "is about the only thing Joe Hardy is letting me keep." He had said no to her heavy walk and her attempt at age. "I asked Joe, 'Aren't you worried about age?' and he said, 'No, just be yourself.' Joe cut out all my creativity," she protested.

She was particularly unhappy about her first line. If, as Mrs. Franklin, she could look to Harry for a response after she heralded herself with "Well, I'm here," and then get none, she felt that she could "go around being mad" throughout the play. "But Joe Hardy told me, 'Don't look at him, don't pay any attention to him. Say the lines and get off.' Joe said he thought it would be corny. Of course it's corny at first. It takes time."

For a week during rehearsals, Barbara was "very upset." Then she asked Hardy again if she could look at Harry. He said, "You can take a split second."

Barbara Lester's concern over the small role of Mrs. Franklin might seem excessive. But she explained to me that it grew out of a respect for the audience she had learned while studying acting at the Berghof Studio, an acting school co-directed by Uta Hagan and Herbert Berghof.

"At the time I went to study with Uta Hagan," Barbara said, "I was ready to quit, because I thought the audience was just a bunch of suckers." Barbara had been working in stock since she was seventeen, and had discovered a number of acting tricks. "If you looked out front, they'd laugh. If you looked sideways, they wouldn't. After I'd done four summers of stock I'd learned five or six of these tricks, and I thought that if I did ten summers of this I'd know sixty tricks. It annoyed me that you could manipulate the audience so easily.

"The most important thing I learned from Uta, and I learned a lot, was respect for the audience. The audience might not know all the little things you know, and they won't all get the same thing. But I realized that no matter how much I knew about the character, the audience would know more, just from seeing it once."

Sada Thompson/Florence. "There are some parts when you know the character right away and you know you can do it right away. There are other parts that other people are convinced you can do, and you're not at all sure. And there are some characters, somewhat like this one, that you feel you can do, but it's a matter of reaching for her, up around that corner she's constantly disappearing around. You just get a glimpse of her, just her skirt or a look or something. It's evasive. However, in your mind there are things about her that you know you're going to get, when you relax into playing and you become more at ease on the stage."

Johnny No-Trump rehearsals were a little under three weeks old as Sada Thompson sat in her dressing room, in a long lamé dressing gown, and prepared rather nervously to go on stage for publicity pictures. "Nazimova, I think, said that the perfect state for an actor was to be like those Chinese bells, those glass bells that are quiescent until a little wind blows them and they make a noise." Sada paused in applying her makeup and fluttered her hand. "You reach that state of relaxation and then things begin to happen out of that. It's almost as if you've implanted something in your brain and suddenly it starts to come to life. This was one of those parts where I had to wait for it to come. It's something you learn to do."

I recalled how frequently Sada Thompson had sat off in the wings, totally immersed in the script. It was obvious that she was working intensely on the role, yet in early rehearsals she sometimes spoke her lines with very little feeling or, apparently, understanding.

"I don't believe in there always being the same method for everything you do," Sada said. "You approach and comprehend each role at a different pace, in a different way. Sometimes you work from the outside in and sometimes from the inside out.

"With this part, I went through it in a kind of textbook way to see what everybody else in the play says about her. How everybody feels about her. Sometimes they'll say something that isn't what they really feel, or at least it's some kind of brusque way of passing off a relationship that is more meaningful.

"It's fairly obvious what she is," Sada said of the character of Florence. "She's a New Yorker, a woman of some aspiration, but a very deeply bourgeois woman, which I appreciate since I am, too. She feels the failure of her marriage. And her son matters terribly to her. I think she tries awfully hard to be a good mother. And she isn't hanging on at all. She tries very hard not to be that way, but when the chips are down she behaves a little differently. Also, the fact that her marriage has failed and the fact that she's living with her brother, not unhappily, but she's living with her brother in this big old house where they both grew up, makes her a little more possessive inside than she thinks she is.

"She has this enormous regard for anybody who achieves something, and she thinks Johnny can achieve anything. But it never occurred to her that he'd want to be a poet. Her one experience being really deeply involved with somebody in the arts was with somebody who didn't have it, or at least she didn't think so. She saw Alec wasting his life and just doomed to be despondent and embarrassed. She can't bear that kind of fate for her boy."

Sada grew up in New Jersey, and enrolled in her first acting class at the age of twelve. "Of course it was all quite superficial," she said. "I dreamed of myself as a big movie star and all that stuff. But I loved playing all kinds of things. I had a great many things to get over, but I certainly had loads of exuberance and vitality." She added, "I also had a tremendous interest in trying to be different kinds of people, and I felt that there were lots of kinds of people in me.

"And I still feel this way. It's a little bit like the way I feel about reading. I love to read—it's almost a vice. I feel as if, in reading, I become acquainted with more people than I could ever hope to meet in life. The same is true in acting."

Sada spoke fondly of one role in particular, which she played during her sophomore year at Carnegie Tech, in Pittsburgh. It was the role of Masha, one of three unhappy sisters in Chekhov's *The Three Sisters,* and it was a landmark for her. "I learned more about acting in that particular production than I've ever been conscious of learning since: taking your time and letting things happen to you, and having some kind of connective tissue that runs through the whole play and supports you through the whole play."

She had finished putting on her makeup and rose to take the dress she would wear as Florence from the clothes rack. She had been rehearsing Florence for three weeks now, and I was beginning to understand what Joe Hardy meant when he said, "She works slowly, but when she cuts loose, she is very, very good indeed."

Tuesday, September 12. Rehearsals went into their second week today. I stopped by the theater around eleven o'clock, a half hour after rehearsal began, and found Pat Hingle and Don Scardino several pages into scene one. Both knew it without their scripts, and with only occasional help from Chuck Kindl, sitting with the promptbook stage left as usual. To my surprise, the scene had changed drastically since I saw it six days before.

Now Johnny and Harry argue darkly and earnestly. Johnny is deliberately getting under Harry's skin, and one can feel the rage boiling up in Harry even before he discovers that Johnny wants to be a poet. Several days ago, the two carried on a noisy, lighthearted argument; now it is all low-voiced, to keep Mrs. Franklin and Nanna from hearing.

Mary Mercier was at rehearsal today, wearing blue jeans and moving restlessly around the house. For a while she sat with Joe Hardy, then by herself a few rows behind him, and then she came down and stopped in the aisle next to my seat. I remarked that the first scene had become more somber. She said, "Maybe this play isn't going to be a comedy. It's a play about a person's spirit being thwarted, and that's not funny."

Thursday, September 14. Today, for the first time, I met two other members of the cast: Bernadette Peters, nineteen years old with a baby-doll voice, granny glasses, and blonde ringlets gathered in a ribbon; and Anne Ives, who was hired after rehearsals began to play the grandmother, Nanna. Like Nanna, Miss Ives is a spirited elderly lady. Her exact age is a secret. "I once told a director my exact age," she mentioned, "and he said, 'I didn't realize you were *that* old.' I didn't get the part. When you get to be eighty, you can start bragging about your age. I'm not far from that mark."

Because her role is a small one, her dressing room is two flights up. But when someone asked if she'd like to change so she would have fewer stairs to climb, she said she could use the exercise.

I had lunch with Anne Ives near the theater, and she told me of her beginnings as an actress, and more remarkable, her rather recent return to the stage.

She first came to New York at sixteen, to study acting at what is now the American Academy of Dramatic Arts. Her first role was in the 1906 production of *The Chorus Lady*. A petite redhead then, Anne Ives played one of the chorus girls.

Then, in 1918, she left New York and the professional theater to take a civil service job in Washington, D.C., in the First World War effort. For thirty years afterward, Anne Ives worked in civil service, while she devoted her evenings to little theaters around Washington. She did dramatic sketches on radio in the days when, to get the sound of traffic, they put the microphone out the window; and her little theater group performed before Constantin Stanislavski when he visited the United States in 1923. Stanislavski sat in the front row, right on top of the actors, but nonetheless examined them through opera glasses. Anne Ives remembered, "He was very gracious. He said all the sorts of things you say when you can't say 'You were wonderful.' "

During these years, Anne had made herself a promise. "I always said, 'When I retire I will go back to the theater.' " In 1947 she did retire, and returned to New York in 1950, to begin again.

Thirty years had changed her, and the New York theater, too. In

1905, vaudeville, melodrama, and serious drama had been thriving, but by 1950 the theater was a business struggling to survive. Yet, though the odds seemed against it, Anne managed to find roles. She toured, worked off-Broadway and in summer stock, regional theater, radio and television. A few months before rehearsals of *Johnny No-Trump* began, she appeared in the movie *The Producers,* starring Zero Mostel. And now there was *Johnny No-Trump.*

"I love the play," Anne said, "and I think the cutting and rewriting Mary has done has been marvelous."

Friday, September 15. It begins to look as though *Johnny No-Trump* really will open in two and a half weeks. When I arrived at the theater this morning, the marquee was emblazoned with *Johnny No-Trump* in bright red script on a sunny yellow background. None of the actors got their names in lights, however—just discreet black print. Sada Thompson, Pat Hingle, and James Broderick are listed above the title, and Don Scardino less conspicuously below. Mary's name is under the title of her play—"A comedy by Mary Mercier." The glass cases have pictures in them now, showing everyone looking a little younger and sleeker than they really are.

Though the trappings outside the theater are ready, the second act has a long way to go. The actors got a script revision today, and were still shuffling typed pages onstage. But the birthday party scene, which has remained just about as written, was beginning to get some fun in it. As Pat Hingle poured the drinks, Don Scardino thrust his glass under the bottle, and Hingle's gruff "get out of there" got a laugh from the audience.

Today's audience included for the first time an envoy from the producers' office, business manager Michael Kasden. Richard Barr was apparently keeping to his policy—hands off for the first two weeks.

After the rehearsal, I had hamburgers with four members of the cast—Sada Thompson, Barbara Lester, Bernadette Peters and Don Scardino—a half block from the theater.

Don Scardino turned the conversation to *Johnny No-Trump.* "Do you think it's going to make it?" he asked the table in general. Barbara Lester was quick to shake her head no. "It doesn't have enough plot," she said. Someone replied that *The Subject Was Roses* didn't have much plot, either, and managed a healthy Broadway run. "Yes," Barbara said, "but the people were affected and changed by each other in that. In this play they don't undergo any real change."

Sada Thompson looked uncomfortable. "I honestly don't know. With modest plays like this one, you never know." Sada was bothered by the wholesale cutting. "The fat needs to be trimmed," she felt, "but when they rewrite whole scenes you lose some of the nuggets, and you find yourself without some of the nice little things."

Chapter 10 The Set Comes In

Midway through rehearsals, on Monday, September 18, while the actors took a day off, the set for *Johnny No-Trump* arrived at the Cort Theater. The set had been built and assembled at a shop near Yankee Stadium. Early that morning, it was loaded piece by piece in trucks and driven to Manhattan for reassembly on the Cort stage. When I arrived shortly after one o'clock, five trucks were parked on either side of Forty-eighth Street, just in front of the theater. Michael Goldreyer, general manager for ABW Productions, stood on the sidewalk surveying the scene, and scowled.

Inside the Cort, the first pieces of the set were beginning to trickle in, carried by stagehands. Hopefully, they would be able to finish their work that night.

Richard Barr was sitting in the center of the house. A few rows behind him was Don Scardino, the only member of the cast there, who said he couldn't stay away. Barr looked on intently. "In a few minutes," he observed, "I'll know whether this is a good crew or not." If they were, he explained, they would position the set pieces along the walls near where they would be on the final set. A few minutes later Barr said, "Yep, they know exactly what they're doing." Grinning widely, he told

Don Scardino, "It's marvelous to watch a show come in."

The stage was filling up. There were twenty-two men in the crew, and one short, round fellow in overalls and a crash helmet cleared the way before him by sounding a high "beep, beep." William Ritman, the designer of the set, stood onstage, watching.

The set was beginning to be recognizable. First came the swinging door, which connects the dining room to a hypothetical kitchen offstage. This door was warm yellow-brown wood, the color of lightly stained oak. "It looks expensive to me," Barr commented, and we all laughed.

Barr, of course, knew what the set was costing him. The design and construction together came to about $10,000. Before the day was over, it would cost him another $1,300, mainly in wages for the crew. By Broadway standards, both sums were very small.

A fake brick fireplace with an ornately carved wooden mantel-piece was being carried across the stage. Pieces of bannister were propped against the upstage wall. Enough of the set was lying around onstage by now to give a feeling of the kind of room it would be—old, comfortable, and woody. "It's going to look almost as good as the model," Barr told Ritman, seeming pleased.

Within an hour the crew had the entire set onstage. Then, simultaneously, one group of men began installing the lights in the back of the house and another assembled the portals and raised them into place. The portals resembled giant black curtain valances. They ran from one edge of the proscenium to the other, to obscure lights and rigging hanging above the stage. It took half a dozen men to hoist each portal up by ropes.

Meanwhile, three of the crew had stationed themselves in the house—one in the orchestra, one looking over the first balcony, and one the second. In this way they formed a human conveyor belt for passing up lights on a rope to the top balcony, where they would beam down on the stage.

Onstage the portals were in place, and the crew readied other lights to hoist above the stage. Pipes were lowered within a few feet of the floor, and then the big, heavy black lights, or lamps, as the men called them, were clamped onto the pipes and lifted. One man was off to the side attaching gel (colored sheets that give stage lights various hues) to other lamps.

Now the most dramatic work of the day, erecting the set, could begin. The house where *Johnny No-Trump* lived emerged piece by piece. A glassless window casement went into place at stage right. Above it was wood trim that resembled the beads of an abacus, and underneath, a wooden window seat. "When Joe Hardy sees that, I bet he'll use that window seat more," Don Scardino said. The fireplace went on the left of the stage, then the swinging door next to it, and then the back wall, complete with bookcases and a cupboard. The walls had been stenciled to simulate wallpaper, which was predominately turquoise.

By 4:45 the walls were up, and the crew was using the kitchen door as if they lived in the house. It was weird, as though they had built a house and moved in all in the same afternoon.

William Ritman, the designer of the set, had begun his work on *Johnny No-Trump* the previous summer. In an interview at his combination studio and apartment, he described how he had gone about it.

"The first thing I do when I'm designing a set," Ritman said, "is read the play and try to get the mood. I think the mood is the most important single thing. Because *Johnny No-Trump* was an intimate show, I wanted a feeling of intimacy in the set. I wanted the room to seem small, but at the same time I wanted the feeling of a big old house."

A big old house would have high ceilings, but to achieve the feeling of height he wanted, Ritman decided to eliminate the ceiling altogether. Instead, he used black portals to define the upper limits of the set.

A feeling of the age of the house was established with what Ritman called "a sort of neo-Victorian style," characterized by a great deal of heavy oak woodwork. "I grew up in an apartment in Chicago that was like the set for *Johnny No-Trump*," Ritman said, "but there was so much woodwork in it that it got to be oppressive. That was one of the problems I faced in designing this set. How do you design a set in an ugly period that isn't in itself ugly? That's a problem a designer often has to solve. With this set, I cut down some on the amount of wood and tried to make the wallpaper not too obtrusive. Also I made the oak less yellow than it usually is in such houses."

In addition to problems of mood and style, Ritman had to meet a number of practical demands imposed by the script. "With *Johnny No-Trump,*" Ritman explained, "a lot was determined by the script. The place—Long Island—was determined, and the grandmother determined that it was an old house. Because of the script, too, there had to be a sort of living room area and a place to eat. And there had to be a staircase."

All of these requirements were incorporated into Ritman's preliminary sketches for the set, though he didn't follow the playwright's specifications entirely.

Once he had a design for the set fairly well in mind, Ritman made a floor plan and met "two or three times" with director Joseph Hardy to discuss it. "Even if he doesn't stage the play ahead of time," Ritman said, "a director has to have some idea of the actor's movements and where the key scenes are going to be played." The staircase, for instance, was "elaborate because Hardy planned to use it a great deal."

The floor plan should be finalized by the time the play goes into rehearsal. It is used by the stage managers when they put down tape on the stage floor, defining the perimeters of the set and marking the approximate placement of various pieces of stage furniture. The tape gives the actors and director a good idea of the space they will have to work in when the actual set arrives.

Once the floor plan is agreed upon, the next step, for Ritman and for most designers, is to build a small model of the actual set. Richard Barr and Mary Mercier saw the set model and Barr had a suggestion about the line of the portals. "But other than that," Ritman said, "this set was pretty much my own."

In the case of *Johnny No-Trump,* Ritman was also designing lighting. Lighting can be extremely complex. Designer Jo Mielziner, for instance, has written that he used 141 lights and 150 light changes during each performance of Arthur Miller's *Death of a Salesman*. On the other hand, lighting for a single-set comedy like *Johnny No-Trump* tends to be relatively simple. "A comedy one-setter," as another lighting designer explained, "is generally lit by a wash of light covering the set so that whichever way the actor turns he is well-lit."

There are usually few changes in the lighting of such a comedy once the curtain goes up. Nonetheless, the lighting designer must draw up a "hanging plot" of the lighting, indicating how many lights he wants and where he wants them. The designer must also draw up detailed, carefully scaled drawings of the set. For, while the set model gives a good idea of what the eventual set will look like, it does not figure greatly in the actual building of the set.

When the time comes to build the set, the role of the set designer on Broadway is quite different than it is elsewhere. In amateur theater, the set designer is likely to be the set builder as well. In regional and repertory theater, the designer may have a shop crew to do the actual sawing and hammering, but he is usually on hand to supervise and perhaps to do some painting on the set. On Broadway, however, the work of building and painting the set is done entirely by one of a few scenic studios. The set for *Johnny No-Trump* was built by Feller Scenery Studios, one of the two largest union shops in New York.

Using the designer's detailed drawings (indicating exact dimensions, wallpaper pattern, wood color, materials, etc.), the scenic studio sets about its work. There are at least four different kinds of work that the shop is required to do on a set: iron work, carpentry, flat scenery construction, and painting.

The process of building a set usually requires from three to four weeks, and throughout the construction, the designer goes to the shop to answer questions and make sure the design is being carried out according to his intentions. The larger studios have complete facilities for erecting the entire set at the shop, and usually do so before they load it piece by piece onto trucks for delivery to the theater.

The long experience and expertise of the scenic studios free the set designer from some worry about technical problems. Peter Feller of

Feller Scenery Studios has said that "the designer, no matter how technically capable he is, is after all an artist, and since we have every dimension . . . of every theater, it is incumbent on us to recheck his specifications and say this will or won't work, or we have to shrink here, or you can't get this unit off stage, or this won't revolve."

Such technical expertise is often a great boon to the designer. Yet, as Ritman explained, the designer sacrifices some of his freedom by working with a scenic studio. "Because of the unions, you have to get the shop to build everything. And anything they build costs $250. Anything! This table," Ritman said, indicating a very small, rickety phone table at his side, "would cost $250. Then on top of that, if you want to put something up, you have to have a call and you can't have a call of less than four hours!

"Everything on Broadway is so expensive that a designer can't make mistakes. If I put up a wall on Broadway and then want to tear it down, I can't because the cost would be prohibitive. A writer at least can see something on stage and then change it if he doesn't like it, but a designer can't." The size of the larger shops (Feller Scenery Studios employs up to 150 workers at peak season) also makes it difficult for the designer to communicate his ideas.

"I'd like to work off-Broadway again," Ritman added, rather wistfully, "but I guess now that I've worked on Broadway, they probably think I'm too expensive." Ritman is one of about eight hundred New York members of United Scenic Artists, a union made up of set and lighting designers who have passed a qualifying examination. By union regulation, he must receive a minimum of $1500 for designing a set on Broadway and $350 for designing a set off-Broadway. Off-Broadway, a set may be built by a non-union shop, either in a loft somewhere or on the stage where the play is to appear. While the work will probably be less expert, it will also be less costly than the work of a union shop. Even off-Broadway, however, many producers choose to deal with union shops.

Since the shops execute most of the sets designed for Broadway and off-Broadway, New York commercial theater is not a good place for a designer to acquire the technical experience he needs. Ritman tends to de-emphasize technical know-how. "What's needed in the theater today is artistry," he said, "not technicians. Anyone can learn the technique. You learn it by doing it."

Yet the fact remains that a designer must "learn it by doing it" at some point in his career, and most young designers acquire this experience outside the New York commercial theater, either at a university or an art school, in stock or in repertory. Ritman, for instance, studied stage design at the Goodman Theater School in Chicago, then designed sets for TV and summer stock before he got his first job off-Broadway, designing Edward Albee's *The Zoo Story* and Samuel Beckett's *Krapp's Last Tape* for Richard Barr in 1960.

Since then, William Ritman has been one of the busiest designers of avant-garde plays in New York. Not only has he designed all but one of Edward Albee's plays, but he has designed sets for the plays of Ionesco and Pinter as well.

Five days before *Johnny No-Trump* opened on Broadway, *The Birthday Party* by Harold Pinter opened down the street, on a set designed by William Ritman. The two sets demonstrate vividly the wide range of mood Ritman is capable of. "With Pinter," Ritman told me, "it's important to let a set breathe. The ideas aren't easy to follow, so the set can't be too complex."

Ritman's set for *The Birthday Party,* like Pinter's strange dialogue, leaves out nearly everything. There are only bare, unadorned gray walls, a staircase and a round table with a few chairs. On the other hand, it is difficult to find a barren square inch on the *Johnny No-Trump* set. Everywhere one looks, there is wallpaper pattern, or woodwork, or a bookcase, or a picture. The house seems busy and full of life even without any actors on the stage.

Chapter 11 Rehearsal Diary: The Third Week

Tuesday, September 19. After two days off, the actors returned today to find real stairs instead of yellow tape on the floor, real doors to slam, and a cushiony sofa to sit on instead of a hard wood bench. They responded with a new intensity. Rehearsal breaks were almost quiet. Pat Hingle, who usually loves to talk, sat silently at the round oak table, and Sada Thompson murmured her lines to herself on the sofa. When the rehearsal ended at nine (rehearsals from now on will start at one and go until nine with a break for dinner), the actors waited in the "living room" for comments from Joe Hardy. "You've fit in fine," he told them. "You look like you live here. Now learn your lines."

Don Scardino mentioned that the producers would come to see a run-through of the play the next day. Pat Hingle was surprised. "Are *they* going to be here tomorrow?" he asked. "Oh ho de oh ho, I'd better go get my script to go over that last scene." Everyone laughed. The producers' arrival put you on your toes.

Wednesday, September 20. The atmosphere at rehearsals during the last two days has been much more tense than before. There is a world of difference between walking through a scene on a bare stage, and walking out from dark wings to do the same scene on a brightly lit set. What's more, the actors waiting backstage for their cues don't have the place to themselves any more, for when the set arrives, so do stagehands. They have put an end to the intimate atmosphere of early rehearsals.

And the arrival of the producers today completed the transformation. Sada Thompson, studying her script on a bench backstage, gave me a smile that said, "Hello, I don't want to talk." Pat Hingle came into the wings still totally engrossed in the scene he'd just left. He leaned against the escape stairs breathing heavily before his next entrance. A stocky young prop man worried over the properties table like a mother hen.

A dinner break followed the run-through. While the actors ate and relaxed, the producers gave Joseph Hardy their verdict on what they had seen.

It was obvious from Joe Hardy's face after the dinner break that the producers had been pleased. "Their reaction was fantastic," he told me, and during the evening rehearsal his exuberance spilled over into his direction. Looking fresh and jazzy in an orange plaid shirt and wide suede belt, he hovered over the actors on stage, urging them to move, to take over, and sometimes kidding them.

He told Bernadette Peters to pose like a model at her entrance. Then he demonstrated—bent his knee and thrust his torso forward like Twiggy. Bernadette broke up.

She and Don Scardino were asked to "take over the stage" during their fight scene. Neither needed much urging. Right away Don hurdled the couch to grab Bernadette, and then she raced upstairs with Don at her heels. Her hair flew, and both of them were in stitches. "Should it turn into the fun we're having with it?" she asked. Joe hesitated. "Yes," he said, and they repeated the scene three times to "set it."

Now Joe turned his attention to act two, scene one. He wanted James Broderick to dominate the stage when he entered. "You can go ape," he told Broderick. "Take over. There are lots of things you can do."

Joe demonstrated. "You come in, you look around the place, you haven't been here since Christmas. It's the same old place. (A disgusted sound.) Look to see if the booze is out. No, it isn't." As the actors ran through Alec's entrance, Joe circled behind them, waving to Jim Broderick to come down right, then left.

Neither James Broderick nor Pat Hingle seemed to share Joe's cheerful appraisal of the run-through. Pat, dressed tonight like a cab driver in a checked sportshirt and red tie, looked tired and older. He told Joe he was worried about a line he didn't think Harry would really address to Johnny: "You'll go to college, although what the hell good that does beats me." Harry would never say that, Hingle felt. "If there's one thing Harry has, it's money tucked away somewhere for the kid's college education. Mary says it's one of the contradictions in Harry but . . ." and his voice trailed off.

James Broderick questioned if there would be time enough to light the candles on Johnny's birthday cake at the party. "That's an awful lot of candles," he said to Hardy, smiling sadly.

Then the director asked a question: "When does Johnny decide *not* to run away?" Hardy believed it was when Harry offered Johnny his trust. Up to then, Johnny plans to leave, and can fight with Bettina because he believes he is going. He has his coat on through most of the first half of act two. But the coat, Hardy felt, was only an *outward* sign of his intention. "It's the *idea* that's important," he said to Don, who nodded in agreement.

The rehearsal over, Pat Hingle sat down in Harry's chair and leaned toward the director. "Did it really go well this afternoon?"

"It was just marvelous," Joe said.

Thursday, September 21. The tense cloud that hung over yesterday's run-through seems to have blown away. Today the actors put in a hard day's work, but they also eased up a bit, taking time out between scenes to talk and joke about things other than *Johnny No-Trump*.

Ideas appeared everywhere. Some were little things that had occurred to the actors between rehearsals. James Broderick suggested that Alec wouldn't sit down immediately after he entered the house, but would stand expectantly until he was sure he wasn't going to get a drink.

Pat Hingle, speaking also of Alec's entrance, imagined that there would be liquor out on the buffet when Alec entered, but that then Harry would slip it into a dresser drawer.

Other changes emerged in action. Sada Thompson told Johnny to stay in school, and then found herself walking over to Harry's chair and picking up an empty coffee cup. This took her by surprise, and she turned to Joe Hardy in the house. "I don't know what I was planning to do with this," she said, holding up the cup.

Joe answered, "Clear the cup and the ashtray too. You're filling it up nicely now. I love it."

There were understudies at rehearsal today, scattered around the house to watch their counterparts onstage. Jim Noble, who was understudy to both Pat Hingle and James Broderick, sat near me and commented, "Understudying is all right if one is in good psychic condition. If one is not, it can be soul-destroying. But it's okay if you're feeling fairly good and working at something else."

I kept hearing Anne Ives's laughter, amazingly like a young girl's, from the recesses of the house, so I walked back to talk with her about the play. "It's gotten so much better with the rewriting," she said. "They've taken out all the unnecessary, nasty things. The grandmother used to say 'snotty,' and I'm so glad they took it out. If I said that as a child, I'd be in trouble. And I don't think Nanna would say it. And I'm so glad they took out some of Nanna's invective at the end of act one, because it slowed down the end of the act. That's something you must never do."

Saturday, September 23. Today two of the three producers—Charles Woodward and Richard Barr, who was dressed in clothes for the country —saw another run-through. (The third producer, Clinton Wilder, is in Europe.) The press agent, Howard Atlee, a man with a melancholy face, and his assistant, Bill Cherry, were also in the audience. And Barbara Lester, after she had finished her scenes, came down to sit out front. When I looked over at her toward the end of the second act, she was lifting her glasses to wipe tears from her eyes.

The performances of Sada Thompson and James Broderick have

flowered in the last three days. During the first two weeks of rehearsal it had seemed that Pat Hingle and Don Scardino would give the strongest performances, but now Sada and Jim, who had both said they must take their time, have become just as strong. Jim Broderick's apologia to Johnny yesterday came across movingly, and Joe Hardy told him it was "real in the best sense." Today, Sada Thompson gave what I thought was her best performance so far. She turned to Johnny after arguing with him and said, "I'm sorry I hit you, baby," with real remorse. "Baby" was not in the script, but later Joe Hardy told her to keep it.

Richard Barr was obviously pleased. As soon as the curtain came down on act one, he strode up the aisle from his seat at the back of the house and grinned widely, looking, with his boots on, like a very happy Paul Bunyan. "Thank God they hit an audience on Wednesday," he called in my direction. "They're so ready for it."

Howard Atlee brought in the *Johnny No-Trump* ad that would appear the next day in the Sunday *New York Times.* Everyone gathered around him to see it, the first ad to appear. Barr was pleased by this, too. "You can read it," he said. "Some of them have so much stuff on them, you can't read them."

There was a meeting after the rehearsal of producers Barr and Woodward, their business manager Michael Kasden, Mary Mercier, Joseph Hardy, and stage manager Don Kohler. It was held at a bar next door to the Cort Theater.

Richard Barr asked Mary Mercier to sit next to him "because you have such a small voice and I want to hear you." Then, after drinks had been ordered, the business began.

Kasden: Do you know the birthday cake is costing us five dollars a night?

Barr (surprised): Five dollars a night! That's forty dollars a week! That's as much as we used to pay some actors. (Laughter.) We'll go along with it for a while, but that seems like a lot. Now, about Bettina's first scene. Can't she remember how she did it in the first reading? I think we should have her play the whole thing sitting down.

(They consult about Bettina's line, "I can't sit because it's bad for my figure." They decide to change it to, "I'll sit, but it's bad for my figure.")

Barr: Her second scene is fine, I think. Except she should pick up on cue. There were three beats before some of her lines.

Hardy: That first scene should build to her fight with Johnny.

Barr: The next directorial point I have is about the father's (Jim Broderick's) entrance. He's too drunk for one thing. It's slow. It should be gayer, happier.

Mercier: He should come in on top.

Hardy: I think the problem boils down to this—he should come on like a star, not a featured player. I think we should pare it down—just a few lines. But the main thing is, he should be a star. He shouldn't defer to anyone.

Mercier: When Harry sells Johnny's poem, he should take off on a spiel. He should be like a Fuller Brush man.

Someone else: Like a barker.

Barr: The boy's marvelous, I think. There's not a false moment in it.

Mercier: He's best in the hardest parts, like when he has to talk about his feelings about Shakespeare.

(After a pause, Barr very calmly raises a question.)

Barr (to Mary): Now . . . how strongly do you feel about Nanna? If you want her in, we'll keep her in.

Mercier (staring at the table): If she goes, then Mrs. Franklin should go, too.

Barr: No, no, Mrs. Franklin is a well-established character.

Hardy: That first scene is marvelous now.

Barr: Nanna's scene delays the entrance of the father (in act two). The audience needs a new figure, a change by then. You have to ask what Nanna adds. I don't feel it adds a new dimension to the play. I feel it is almost a cliché in a play that is relatively free of clichés.

Mercier (seconds later): I think we should try running it without her.

Hardy: Do you think that's necessary? I feel that's so hard on the actors.

Mercier (softly): I hate cutting an actress.

Barr: Oh, I'll have to take care of that. At least we're not cutting her because she's no good, and she'll know that. I've had to do that many times.

Hardy: When would be the best time to tell her?

Barr: I'll call her tomorrow (Sunday).

Hardy: I'd like to call her, too. And I'll call the other actors and tell them, since they're such a close bunch.

I was stunned. Although the idea must have been discussed before, this was the first inkling I'd had that white-haired Anne Ives, so clearly elated by her Broadway role, wasn't going to play Nanna after all. I remembered what Anne had said at lunch the week before: "I told my agent I wanted to play one more Broadway role, then this came along."

Mary Mercier was the only one who was openly glum about it. The rest of the table discussed the coming week matter-of-factly. Monday off, a technical rehearsal to try out costumes and test lights on Tuesday, and on Wednesday, a dress rehearsal before an invited audience—people invited by the cast. The party scene needed more inner energy, Joe Hardy said; perhaps they could turn on a radio?

"Yeah," said Mary unhappily, "and the announcement will come over the radio that World War III has just begun."

After everyone else had left, she murmured softly, "I hate firing actors. It's the most brutal part of this business."

At the evening rehearsal, the actors discussed props and costumes in the set living room. None of them knew yet that Anne Ives was going to be cut from the play. They talked briefly at one point about Sada Thompson's shoes. Anne Ives asked Joe Hardy about her own shoes. Were the heels perhaps too square? Joe Hardy looked at her shoes for a second and answered, "No, those will be just fine."

When I saw Anne Ives at a preview performance of *Johnny No-Trump* ten days later, she appeared almost totally recovered. She wore a lace dress and brocaded hat, and greeted me with a joke. "Now you have something to put in your book."

I asked her how she was feeling, and she was momentarily somber. "My heart's up from the bottom of the ocean now." She spoke of the play with admirable generosity. "I think it's going very well, don't you?"

Chapter **12** Rehearsal Diary: The Last Twelve Days

Tuesday, September 26. A week ago I heard Bill Ritman tell Richard Barr that he had only one costume for *Johnny No-Trump*. Yet somehow or other, during the last week, costumes have been put together so that today, when the photographers arrived, everyone had something in character to wear. In some cases, the transition from everyday dress to costume is hardly noticeable. James Broderick usually wears a suit and tie to rehearsals, and he will wear a suit and tie as Alec. Don Scardino's costume consists of blue jeans with holes in both knees, an army fatigue jacket, and a cowboy hat—all his own. He has a number of buttons pinned to the hat, and among them is one that reads "poet." It did not come from Don's collection.

One night, Joe Hardy had been riding home from the theater in a cab and noticed the "poet" button on the windshield. He explained to the driver that he was directing a play about a cab driver and his young nephew who wants to be a poet. The cab driver said, "You know, I've had that button up there for two years, but I think I'm gonna give it to you."

In addition to presenting Don with the "poet" button, Joe Hardy also assigned him a barber who specializes in cutting actors' hair. The barber had his orders, and when Don arrived at the shop he lost perhaps two inches of red hair, but the remainder is thick and shaggy enough to keep him looking with-it. Glassless hornrims, in which he has been rehearsing for some time now, complete the costume. Don doesn't wear glasses offstage, but now says he feels naked onstage without them.

Pat Hingle, on the other hand, needs glasses offstage, but has begun to wear contact lenses for this play. He himself finds it difficult to see facial expressions across a stage, but thought Harry probably wouldn't wear glasses, so he decided to try contacts. They have been giving him some trouble, and I think he tends to squint with them, but as Harry is a worrier, it seems appropriate.

For the photographers today, Hingle was wearing rumpled cotton pants, a plaid cotton shirt open at the neck, and a cardigan sweater with two buttons buttoned but looking as though they were about to pop. Pat Hingle isn't much overweight, but the posture he adopts as Harry, plus the tight sweater, create the illusion of a sizeable paunch.

His costume is flattering, however, compared with Barbara Lester's. She wears a droopy apron, old shoes, and a huge cardigan that might have been left behind by one of Mrs. Franklin's male boarders. White anklets are the final touch.

Sada Thompson's costume is soft and pretty—a gray flared skirt and a pink sweater set worn with three strands of pearls. For act two, she wears a green knit dress.

Bernadette Peters's costume is a copy of a department store dress. Bernadette and Bill Ritman shopped for it together. The dress is turquoise with two little pockets ("And there's two pockets, and here's a kerchief to match," Bettina says in the play), and a dark ribbon trim around the hem and down the long sleeves. But the tip-off to Bettina's personality is less her dress than her hairdo. Usually Bernadette gathers her blonde hair in ringlets at the back of her head; for this part, she has teased it into a high bouffant, all except for one silly curl cemented with an equally silly turquoise bow to the side of her face. As Bettina loses her composure during her fight with Johnny, the hairdo begins to fly. This was accidental at first, but has now become a nightly event.

While the actors were in their dressing rooms putting on costumes and makeup for the publicity photographs, other people were working busily on the set. The production propertyman was telephoning to buy another set of binoculars for Johnny. Merrily Mossman, Joe Hardy's assistant, had combed junk shops for old pictures for the living room, and was admiring one of her finds, a framed snapshot of glum-faced newlyweds. And Lee Parker, the wardrobe mistress, trimmed the lace tablecloth that would cover the round oak table.

The flurry of preparation was not all for the photographers. It was also for tomorrow night's preview audience. There will be six by-invitation previews, essentially dress rehearsals before a small audience of friends. Members of the company have been asked to sign their friends up for tickets on bulletins posted in the hall outside the dressing rooms, and to distribute the tickets themselves. I noted today that most of the cast is playing it safe by inviting friends to later, rather than earlier previews.

Wednesday, September 27. This evening *Johnny No-Trump* had an audience for the first time. It was a young group, undoubtedly forewarned when they received their tickets not to expect a finished performance.

There were other reminders that tonight was a dress rehearsal. The sound of a hammer making a last minute adjustment on the set penetrated the curtain. A moment later someone tested the doorbell. Just before the curtain rose, Richard Barr strode confidently to the front of the stage and then abruptly turned shy and awkward. His voice cracked like a boy's as he welcomed the audience.

Perhaps because of the audience, Pat Hingle and Don Scardino appeared to be straining during the first scene. Harry's true character, which Hingle had projected so beautifully early in rehearsals, was obscured tonight by attempts to woo the audience. Don seemed to be over-embellishing Johnny, too. "I couldn't think of any two people I'd less rather spend an evening with," I heard someone in the audience complain at intermission. "I can't stand the boy or his uncle."

Surprisingly enough, the second act, which everyone had been worried about, seemed to play better. Bernadette Peters's first scene drew applause. The ending of the play appeared to move the audience, and after the final curtain, several people were wiping tears from their eyes.

Friday, September 29.   Charles Woodward told me this morning that a major change will be made in the play, probably tonight. It was suggested by Richard Barr after last night's preview.

Woodward explained what the change would be: in the original version, a fairly long time elapses during which the audience, Harry, and Alec know that Johnny's mother is dead, while Johnny does not know. Alec is alone with Johnny for a time, while Harry is at the hospital, but he is unable to tell Johnny what has happened. Instead he makes a long and moving apology to Johnny for his drinking and his failure as a father and husband. Only when Harry returns does Johnny learn of his mother's death.

Woodward and others felt that last night's audience became impatient waiting for Johnny to learn the truth, so Barr suggested this remedy: Alec will make his apologia before Florence dies, earlier in the script when Johnny asks him the questions, "Why do you drink? Why'd you marry my mother?" Later, when the hospital telephones, Alec will volunteer to go, telling Harry to "stay and take care of your kid." Then, in a few short sentences, Harry will tell Johnny of his mother's death, and the curtain will come down.

The actor most affected by this change was James Broderick, and he was not as convinced as Barr and Woodward that it will improve the play. "They're worried about the audience feeling uncomfortable at the end and thinking, 'When are they going to tell Johnny?' " Broderick said, "but I see no reason for the audience to feel comfortable at that point. There's no need to have a tight, neat little ending to the play."

James Broderick was also concerned about the acting problem the change would present. "You just don't talk about a person the same way when she's dead as when she's alive." He would have to adapt in twenty-four hours, between one preview and the next, and he was balking at the lack of time. In the end, despite protestations, Broderick made the change successfully for this evening's performance.

Despite the worry about the second act, Pat Hingle and Don Scardino threw over much of their self-consciousness of two nights before, and played their scene in act one more as I had seen and loved it in rehearsals. The audience seemed to enjoy it, too. When Johnny ran out into the rain in pajamas, they drowned out his rendition of "Singing in the Rain" with enthusiastic applause. After that, the play glided smoothly through act one, and surprisingly, through the shifts in act two.

The most pleased member of the audience may well have been Richard Barr. "I think we've got it licked now," he said. "In a couple of days, we'll freeze it, but not quite yet."

Tuesday, October 3. Opening night is now five days away, and tomorrow the first paid preview audience will see the show. Joe Hardy, however, does not regard the deadline as reason for stepping up rehearsals. He did not call a rehearsal on Saturday or Sunday, and gave the actors Monday off. There was no invited preview last night, and today, instead of working onstage, Joe devoted a good part of the afternoon to sessions with actors in their dressing rooms. I, too, visited several of the actors, curious to see if they shared Joe Hardy's apparent confidence about the opening.

Don Scardino's dressing room is on the first floor—this because he is considered a lead, and according to Broadway tradition and Equity ruling, the larger an actor's role, the better his quarters.

When I talked to Don three weeks before, he hadn't been sure yet how well he was doing. "My problem," he lamented then, "is that I have no gauge to tell whether I'm good or not. A lot of people *can* tell, or seem to be able to, anyway. I can't tell, I just go out there and do it."

Today, perhaps because he had sensed the warm response of the preview audiences to his performance, Don appeared more nervous than seriously worried. At the start of his career, he has a great deal at stake in *Johnny No-Trump,* and will be greatly affected by the reviews this coming Sunday night. "I feel a lot of pressure right now," he told me, "because I'm working harder than I ever have before. And also, I'm laying myself wide open career-wise."

Don had covered his dressing room walls with posters and pictures. Bob Dylan and Ravi Shankar were there, and the Beatles, in a poster reprint of the album cover for *Sergeant Pepper's Lonely Hearts Club Band*. On the door were street signs for Haight-Ashbury in San Francisco. Don had hung up three of his own drawings: one was called "Visionary," and had a figure with colored rays streaming from its eyes. There was also an anti-war poster which pictured Lyndon Johnson standing on a Viet Cong soldier.

Don is in tune with his generation in some ways, yet he is aware of many ways in which he is different. "I have trouble getting along with kids my age, because children in this business grow up very fast. When you're on the road, you have to fend for yourself. You see things in people that you wouldn't see otherwise. It can be seamy sometimes. And you're making a lot of money and have responsibility as far as the money's concerned. All my close friends in the neighborhood where I grew up, except for one, sort of seem ill-at-ease with me now. It's sad, but you have to choose your life and the way you want to be. And you make new friends."

Don still lives with his family in the two-apartment building in Queens where he grew up. His parents are both musicians and are enthusiastic about his career, although they were not involved when Don started out five years ago, touring with *Critic's Choice*. When he came home from that tour, he went to a regular public high school for six months and hated it. "It wasn't that I was special, I'd tasted this other life."

Don was getting more work in theater by then, and decided to go to a school for professional children. Such professional schools are geared to young people with careers in show business and other arts, and classes usually last from nine in the morning until one, leaving afternoons free for auditions, rehearsals, modeling, and the like.

By now Don had begun to earn as much, if not more, than his parents. Particularly lucrative was his two-year stint on *The Guiding*

Light. The pay scale for any actor in soap opera is $165 for each half-hour show, and Don says, "It gets so money has very little value because you make so much of it."

One problem which he shares with many nineteen-year-olds weighed heavily on his mind. Don had been classified 1A and was eligible for the draft. He was strongly against the war in Vietnam. "I'm perfectly willing to spend two years of my life in national service—in the Peace Corps, in Vista—to build constructively. But I can't see going over to this war-weary little country and imposing my way of life on its people. But tomorrow I could get a letter, and in two weeks I could be in the army."

Don sometimes finds acting a way of not thinking about this. "I don't know if it's a danger or not, but acting to me is an escape. As a matter of fact, about six months ago when I was having a lot of trouble with the army, I found myself more attached to my girlfriend in the soap opera, and my parents in the soap opera, than my girlfriend and parents in real life. When I was on the soap opera, all the worries that Don Scardino had weren't there. And now when I get onstage, I become John Edwards. And John Edwards isn't worrying about the army or my girlfriend or my parents or money. He's worrying about John Edwards."

Within minutes after I had left his dressing room, I heard Don begin to play his guitar. I went on to talk to Pat Hingle in his dressing room.

Most of the dressing rooms had wall mirrors, but Pat's had only a small mirror, in a corner over his dressing table. There was also a cot without bedding. A pair of socks had been hung up to dry over a small sink. I wondered if Pat Hingle had washed the socks himself, or if this was part of his "dresser's" job. Pat was required to have a dresser by union rules, yet it was hard to imagine what one could do for him, since his costume was a simple sportshirt and cotton pants.

Pat asked if I had read Walter Kerr's article in the *New York Times* the previous Sunday. I had. It was headlined "Maybe This Year, Maybe," and in it, Walter Kerr expressed wonder that this fall, as happened at the start of each year's theater season, energy, hope, and money were poured into Broadway productions that were, for the most part, destined to fail.

Despite the fact that three out of four plays that open on Broadway flop, Pat felt optimistic about *Johnny No-Trump.* One reason was Don Scardino. "It would have been difficult for me had Don not been such a lovable boy. It would have been hard for me to carry the great love and warmth that Harry has for the boy, covered by this façade of gruffness."

Offstage, Pat Hingle and Don Scardino had often expressed their affection for each other through kidding. Don called Pat "old Dad," a nickname that Pat, at forty-three, accepted with a comical wince.

My own feeling was that the warmth between Don and Pat had spilled over into their performances onstage, perhaps to the detriment of the play. This was particularly true of the first scene, where Harry and Johnny argue. As a member of the cast observed, "They're having so much fun with the first scene that they're not really fighting any more."

Today I asked Pat Hingle how and when the first scene had become so playful. "When we first started working," Hingle answered, "I had decided that Harry likes to read the morning paper. If he's read the *Daily News,* he's fulfilled his responsibility as a good citizen. Then, maybe later on in the day, he'll drop a little homily that he's gotten from the paper, or draw a moral from it. Or if someone mentions Vietnam, he'll be able to say something about it. So when the kid comes down the stairs, Harry is trying to read the paper and the kid is bothering him by keeping him from it."

Done this way, however, the encounter between Johnny and Harry in the first scene became so disagreeable it was not good for the play. "One of the things we've learned about this play," Hingle explained, "is that any choices we make, however real, that get too much 'lower depths' are bad for the play. This is basically a humorous play, and yet we've got the death of a major character at the end. Harry's first lines to the boy are pretty rough: 'You up? You're gonna be late for school. Take yourself a walk. Eat your breakfast,' " he snapped off.

To better reveal the love that exists between Harry and Johnny, Hingle tried something different. "Now when the kid comes down, Harry has already read the newspaper. He's waiting for the kid to come down to start the game—a game Harry and the kid play every morning. Harry plays the fall guy, and the kid plays the sharp comic.

Chuck Kindl leaned in. "Mr. Hingle," he said respectfully, "they want you onstage."

Joe Hardy was working with the two young people onstage. First he had Don run through the final scene of the play, when Johnny learns of his mother's death. He reminded him to "work on that thing I told you about." Don did the scene apparently more to his satisfaction, and Hardy turned out toward me in the house. "That scene's been worrying me all weekend. He doesn't feel anything because he's never experienced death."

He turned to Bernadette Peters, and went over her lines as she tells Harry and Alec of Florence's death. He wanted Bernadette to face front on the key words so that the audience would be sure to hear them.

There were signs of nerves at rehearsal today. When Sada Thompson came onstage, she immediately focused on a place mat on the dining room table. "That's edging over again," she said nervously, and shifted it a fraction of an inch.

Joe Hardy gave her a reassuring hug. "Don't worry about the props dear."

She laughed, "It keeps me from worrying about everything else."

Later I learned that Sada was also uncomfortable with the tuna fish sandwiches she and Harry ate for lunch in the first act. They were so thick and dry, it seems, that she had trouble saying her lines after she took a bite.

Despite everyone's worries, the preview tonight went well. Whatever Pat Hingle and Don Scardino are doing in their first scene, the audience is responding as it hadn't in early previews. Tonight there was applause when Johnny ran out on "Singing in the Rain."

Saturday, October 7. I stayed away from the first three paid previews on the assumption that a little time off from *Johnny No-Trump* might give me a fresh viewpoint. I returned eager to see how the production had changed. My curiosity was not shared, however, by Mary Mercier, who was standing at the back of the theater, unable even to watch the show. "I feel like a mother whose kid is down in a mine somewhere and they're trying to get him out," she said.

I watched act two. The audience was enthusiastic at the final curtain, and I heard one woman, filing out, say, "The acting was good." A man commented to his wife, "The father was miscast, but I liked the play." In the ladies' room, one matronly woman told another, "That ending's too morbid. That's why I go to the movies, I don't like morbid endings."

According to business manager Michael Kasden, who keeps track of ticket sales, the size of the paid-preview audiences has grown dramatically each succeeding night. Because there has been little advance publicity, this fact can only mean that word has gotten around that *Johnny No-Trump* is worth seeing. Yet, though the growing audiences are good for the cast's morale, everyone in the company is aware that on Broadway, "word-of-mouth" is not enough to keep a play alive. Largely because of the economic situation on Broadway, the success or failure of *Johnny No-Trump* will be determined by the reaction of newspaper and television critics to the opening performance tomorrow night.

Producer Charles Woodward told me that "if we get good notices and we don't get an immediate reaction from the public, we'll do a lot of advertising, everything we can to keep the show open. If we get poor notices, we'll close the show. Very few plays in the history of the American theater, no matter who was in the cast and no matter how much money they spent on advertising, have survived poor notices. It's more true now than ever before."

Because of the cost of tickets, Woodward explained, audiences will not take chances on a show unless it has received critical raves. And because of the cost of production, producers cannot afford to keep a show open without sizable audiences.

Actually, by Broadway standards, *Johnny No-Trump* had been an inexpensive show. Woodward estimated that it cost $42,000 cash and $16,000 in bonds to open the first paid preview. Because the play had neither a name author nor big stars in the cast, it was expected to lose money during the four nights of paid previews. By tonight, despite increasing ticket sales for the previews, the cost of *Johnny No-Trump* had risen to $81,000.

According to Woodward, it was still "probably one of the cheapest shows produced in years. Nothing will come in as cheap this year, or maybe ever again, because the cost of things has gone up and up and up."

A principal factor in the spiraling costs are the demands of the stagehands' union. "You try to engineer a show so that you don't need a lot of extra stagehands," Woodward said. But even *Johnny No-Trump*, with its small cast and single set, hadn't entirely avoided featherbedding. "We had to get a special man to handle the rain effect," Woodward noted. "The rain effect is on as the curtain goes up. We have several people who could easily turn that thing on, but we had to have a special man."

It had been easier to cut corners in other areas. The set was relatively inexpensive, and the advertising budget was low. "We have not spent a great deal of money on advertising because nobody knows the show—it's a sleeper. And I agree with Dick Barr and Clinton Wilder that advertising way in advance is a waste of money, unless you're selling a lot of tickets for one of the big names.

Johnny No-Trump, Woodward thought, would get good reviews, and "do very good business for quite some time. I don't think we're a sellout play, but I figure we could have a nice run. At capacity we can take in $47,000 a week in ticket sales. But we can actually break even if we gross around $18,400 or $18,500. So I feel this play will get good notices, the public will like it, and I figure we should have a nice run, grossing in the area of thirty to forty thousand."

What would happen if the notices were mixed? "It depends on who does it to us. For our particular show, the most important reviews are the *New York Times,* CBS, and NBC. Because of the lack of papers in New York, the television stations have taken on a new importance. If the *Times* gives us good notices and we get bad reviews from other papers, that's fine. If CBS, NBC, and the *New York Times* give us good notices, we have a hit. If they don't, no one can save us."

At least one critic, Clive Barnes of the *New York Times*, feels producers over-emphasize the power of the critics. "I think people put far too much stress on the power of the critics," he told me. "I think critics only have power when they come out and say, 'This is absolutely the most marvelous thing, go and steal tickets and knock old ladies down at pedestrian crossings in your eagerness to get to the theater. This is the greatest play I've seen in two weeks.' Those kinds of notices, what are called stunning notices, I resolutely refuse to write. Those have some kind of effect, it seems, although I think after a time their effect is diluted, when people go to see these great works of art and find out they're not so great after all."

Clive Barnes came to New York from London in 1965 to become dance critic for the *Times*. This season, he took on drama criticism as well. "Ever since I've taken this job," he told me, "I've tried desperately hard to get away from this American concept of judgment. I believe a critic should be more an advocate than a judge. I've tried to let my prejudices become apparent and all the time stress fallibility. I'm appalled at the idea that the critic's opinion is better than the next man's, or that there's some sort of divinity that attaches to it.

"The critic should have a very informed opinion, of course. It's not of much interest to have someone who's seen *Hamlet* for the first time say, 'This is the best *Hamlet* I've seen in my life.' It's also the worst he's ever seen, so that doesn't mean much. But fundamentally the critical function is not to judge but to stimulate, to stimulate interest in the theater as much as in any individual play, to try and make people think that the theater is an interesting, lively thing which may offer them something.

"I don't care if they throw my review across the floor and say, 'the man's an idiot.' That's fine. The point is to make them think about the theater rather than digest opinions, which I think is depressing."

Clive Barnes admitted that he sometimes makes remarks in reviews which he later regrets, and attributed this partly to his deadline. As a rule, an opening lets out around ten. He has until eleven-thirty to complete a review. "Now this is insane in a way," Barnes said. "Producers spend an enormous amount of money, and take these enormous chances, and then they expect a sort of penny-in-the-slot judgment. I must say, however, that you do get used to this. What is it Dr. Johnson said? 'Nothing clears the mind so quickly as the thought of imminent execution.' And when you've got this deadline you *do* think."

Tomorrow night from about ten to eleven-thirty, Clive Barnes will be at the *Times* office, thinking, for better or for worse, of *Johnny No-Trump*.

Chapter **13** Opening Night

Try as one might, it was impossible to forget the critics on opening night. Not only was the curtain scheduled to rise at seven rather than eight-thirty, so that they could meet their newspaper and television deadlines, but although the critics weren't among the crowd gathered under the theater marquee when I arrived, the tuxedoed presence of the press agent, Howard Atlee, and his assistant, Bill Cherry, near the curb was a reminder that they were on their way. Howard and Bill would wait outside until every last critic had passed before giving word that the curtain could rise.

As for the critics, they would arrive at the last possible moment and take aisle seats for an easy escape after the final curtain. For them, this opening was just another night's work.

The crowd lingering under the bright lights of the marquee obviously felt differently. Some had dressed formally, in tuxedos and long gowns, and were making a gala evening of it. They had come to be seen, as well as to see a play. Others simply enjoyed the parade of faces and searched the crowd eagerly for celebrities.

Onstage, signs of opening-night nerves were everywhere during scene one, at least to someone who had watched the play many times before. Pat Hingle turned the pages of the *Daily News* so violently that they were mangled by the time he was through. And at one point in the scene, Don Scardino's poetry notebook flew out of his hand, landed downstage, and lay there distractingly. It had been days since Don had forgotten a line, but after he told Harry, "Take a letter," several hair-raising seconds passed when I thought he wasn't going to remember what came next.

Barbara Lester got a laugh on the opening line of the play, "Well, I'm here." This was a line she had worried about. Yet the simple act of closing a door behind her on her exit a few seconds later, which I doubt she'd ever worried about, presented a problem. She felt behind her for the doorknob, couldn't find it, and finally had to turn around and look for it.

These were small things. The audience probably missed them entirely, sensing only an excess of energy on the stage. By scene two, the actors were in control, and the audience became increasingly enthusiastic. They greeted the curtain on act one with strong applause.

I knew Mary Mercier was waiting out opening night in the bar next door to the theater, and I walked over to talk with her during intermission. The bar was crowded with first-nighters, all in high spirits. The only pocket of cheerlessness in the place was Mary's booth. An actor friend was sitting next to her with his arm around her shoulder.

As I made my way toward them, Bertha Case passed me, heading in the same direction. "I think it's going very well, don't you?" she said, hurrying on, her full satin coat cutting a wide swath.

Mary's voice was as noncommittal as her face. She looked suspended.

As the crowd began to drift back to the theater, I heard a young man in a tuxedo say to his date, "You've got to see the second act. It's my act." And act two, which had been worried over and revised far more than the first, proved to be everyone's act tonight.

There was a tense moment when, for no apparent reason, a dish fell from a shelf and broke on the floor. But Pat Hingle rose to the occasion, walked over to investigate the damage, and without losing the continuity of the scene, kicked the pieces out of the way.

The birthday party had real gaiety, and the audience stayed with the play right through the tragic ending. At the final curtain, as the critics rushed up the aisles and off to write their notices, the audience rose and shouted bravos.

There was a cast party at Joe Hardy's townhouse on West Seventy-eighth Street following the performance. When I arrived, everyone had gathered downstairs in a room crowded with three television sets and a bed full of coats. Mary Mercier was seated a few feet from the televisions, still in her coat, and her face looked blank.

Dick Barr was talking excitedly in the midst of the crowd. "We've already gotten two good radio reviews. One compared it to *Ah Wilderness.*" As WNEW news seemed to be ending and the theater review about to come on, he added, "Television is very important to us now."

The review, however, did not come at once. First a commercial, then the weather report, then a lecture on human reproduction. Finally, the newscaster introduced Stewart Klein, who would review "a rare Sunday night opening."

Everyone held their breath, and he began, "*Johnny No-Trump* is a beautiful play."

A roar went up from the group, followed by "shushes" as the praise continued. The play was "witty and intelligent . . . poignant and tragic . . . a genuinely moving experience." Mary Mercier had "an unerring ear for dialogue," and Pat Hingle had given "the performance of his career." Finally, Stewart Klein summed up by calling *Johnny No-Trump* "a winner. And it may be a winner again when the Tony awards are given out."

Everyone in the room was gleeful except Mary, who rose silently and took her coat off.

"Are you going to stay now, Mary?" someone asked.

"I have my coat off, don't I?" she answered. For the first time in days I saw a glint of pleasure in her eyes. She added cautiously, "I'll stay for a little while, anyway, let's put it like that."

Just then Pat Hingle passed the door, and someone shouted to him, "They say you gave the performance of your lifetime!"

Pat grinned and fumbled for a reply. "Well, that's . . . that's always good to hear."

Despite the sound of a rock-and-roll record in the background and the rave review the play had just received, the guests circulating about the large room upstairs were subdued. Sada Thompson, who was there with her husband, had an almost sad smile on her face. Joe Hardy nursed his drink and spoke calmly about the history of his townhouse. Michael Kasden had shed his bow tie and the jacket of his tuxedo, and changed to tennis shoes, but otherwise seemed as usual.

It was nearly time for the next review, and the crowd began to gravitate toward the television sets again.

Downstairs, Don Scardino had blocked Bertha Case's view of the screen, and she asked him to sit down. Don replied that the reviews weren't on yet. Miss Case appeared nervous and was chain smoking. Finally Edwin Newman of NBC appeared to review *Johnny No-Trump,* and Don sat down.

The review was favorable, although it was not a rave like the first had been. Edwin Newman had reservations about the plot, and felt that Mary Mercier took an "easy way out" with the ending. But she was "a playwright with a future" and had written "the first interesting American play of the Broadway season." He also praised the cast.

Next came Leonard Harris on CBS. His review was less favorable than Newman's, although he commended the "strong professional performances" and said Mary Mercier had shown that she could "create characters." But he continued, "Next time she must create more of a play for them."

Someone in the crowd asked Richard Barr a question everyone had on their minds: "What's the verdict?"

"So far I think we're positive," Barr answered. He added a little formally, "We've been doing this for years. Let us handle it."

Bertha Case was upset after the CBS review. "Did you understand this review?" she asked, her accent noticeable in the excitement. "I didn't understand a word of it."

But there was worse in store. Alan Jeffries of ABC called the play a cliché. "The boy wants to be a poet—don't we all?" he quipped. He had liked the acting, and particularly Don Scardino. "Don Scardino holds his own with Pat Hingle, and since Pat Hingle is one of my favorite actors I mean that for mighty high praise indeed." But the last line of his review was, "Remember Don Scardino, forget *Johnny No-Trump*."

Reactions came swiftly. Don's father had reason to be proud, and turned to me: "I feel like bursting a few buttons. I can't help it," he said. But Don's reaction was subdued. "I feel like the villain."

Mary Mercier told Bertha Case that she was going to give up play-writing and go back to auditioning. Everyone protested. Bertha Case recalled the bad reviews Tennessee Williams had received after his first play opened in Boston. "I told him, this is a moment to grow up in."

Clearly, because of the mixed nature of the television reviews, it all depended now on what Clive Barnes wrote in the *Times*. The Barnes review became the unspoken preoccupation of everyone, though some, including Pat Hingle and Sada Thompson, didn't stay to see it.

At close to twelve-thirty in the morning, Howard Atlee climbed up the stairs with several copies of the next day's *Times* under his arm. I felt a tinge of dread as I saw the serious expression on his face. He handed Richard Barr a copy of the newspaper, opened to the review. Everyone gathered around, and Barr glanced over it. "It's all right," he said. This seemed to mean that it could be read aloud, and he proceeded to read it.

Theater: Misfit at Odds With World

'Johnny No-Trump' in Premiere at Cort

By CLIVE BARNES

THE critic's life would be greatly simplified if there were only two kinds of play —the good and the bad. But in fact plays stubbornly refuse to admit such a categorization, and only people with a "hit-or-miss" mentality are foolish enough to impose on themselves and us what can never be natural. Plays are not to be dismissed as either a hit or miss—and producers should possibly ponder over this a little.

Mary Mercier's "Johnny No-Trump," which came to the Cort Theater last night, cannot be characterized as either good or bad. In fact, if I had to summarize it with one word I'd be tempted to call it schizophrenic. For there are times when the characters (it is beautifully acted, incidentally) seem to be talking with absolute truthfulness, but the moment passes, and within seconds the play has changed gear and is offering what, especially by comparison, is nothing more than slick gibberish.

•

Miss Mercier (it is a first play, by the way) has taken a cliché, and now and again embroidered it with truth. The latter does not forgive the former, but it certainly helps. First for the cliché: This is the 16-year-old misfit at odds with his parents and the world. Here he is a fresh kid who wants to become a drop-out and a poet. Brought up by a wise-cracking yet school marmish mother and a reactionary lump of an

uncle, the boy appears to be going to take after his divorced father — a painter, wastrel and alcoholic.

The strains of hearts and flowers are never far away from this orchestra pit, and when the author solves her problem of a suitable ending with a death far too melodramatic for the theater (only real life normally can get away with such random coups de théâtre) she lost a certain amount of my sympathy.

Miss Mercier's difficulty seems to be that while she knows how people really speak, she is unable to heighten dialogue consistently for the theater. Usually she went too far so that her people sounded like any other synthetic theatricals. Something of her own realization of this emerged toward the end, when one of the characters said: "Why does a for-real feeling always come out as corn." This is a problem for Miss Mercier's next play.

•

Where the play did succeed, unequivocally I thought, was in its staging and acting. Joseph Hardy, a distinguished refugee from Off Broadway on his first Broadway assignment, does wonders, not only in giving a fundamentally mechanical play a genuine air of spontaneity, but also in finding the rare but special passages when the characters sound as if from life rather than romantic fiction, and gently underscoring them.

Pat Hingle is the kind of actor who can wring out the truth from the blandest commonplace, and given a role that demanded nothing more than gruff lovability, he played it as if it had the di-

mensions of a role by Ibsen. Almost as good (although her role did not have the same temptations for crass syrup as did Mr. Hingle's) was Sada Thompson as the boy's mother, a portrayal that suggested a depth of reality and pain far beyond the conventional sweet and sour writing of the dialogue.

As the boy, Don Scardino had the difficulty of an unconvincing role, seeming both surprisingly mature and unbelievably unsophisticated often in the same speech. For this fresh kid with an antic disposition and a tongue that sounded as if it had been plucked out of a stand-up comic's scriptwriter, could have been unsympathetic, and Mr. Scardino played him with charm and aplomb. James Broderick was also happily efficient as the painter-father, slightly drunk, completely weak, but not altogether unendearing.

•

So there it is. A cliché play at heart, yet one with good enough passages and strong enough (if rickety) architecture to support a sextet of good players. I personally would have preferred to have written it than, say, "Cactus Flower," but that does not mean it will run as long.

The Cast

JOHNNY NO-TRUMP, a play by Mary Mercier. Staged by Joseph Hardy; setting, lighting and costumes by William Ritman; production stage manager, D. W. Koehler. Presented by Theater 1968 (Richard Barr, Clinton Wilder, Charles Woodward Jr.). At the Cort Theater, 138 West 48th Street.

Harry Armstrong	Pat Hingle
Mrs. Franklin	Barbara Lester
John Edwards	Don Scardino
Florence Edwards	Sada Thompson
Alexander Edwards	James Broderick
Bettina	Bernadette Peters

Michael Kasden was still mulling over another copy of the *Times* as Barr finished. Bertha Case stood behind Mary, stroking her hair. Across the room, Joe Hardy looked blank. I had glanced at him earlier when Barr read the praise of his direction, and he had rolled his eyes toward the ceiling in disgust. Don Scardino, near the fireplace, met my gaze and smiled sadly.

"Well, it's a bad review folks," Barr said. "I'm sorry." Bertha Case protested, but Barr repeated, "Don't kid yourselves—it's a bad review."

The party broke up quickly and quietly. I asked Charles Woodward what the review meant. "It all depends on what Watts (the *New York Post* critic) and Chapman (the *Daily News*) say tomorrow."

At the top of the staircase I listened to Mary Mercier speaking to Bertha Case below. Her words hung in the air. "What right have they to criticize? I only do it as a hobby. Anything else I write will be put away on a shelf." Bertha Case prodded her gently toward the door.

Joe Hardy watched them leave, from the top of the stairs, and said, "That's when it's really bad, when people work hard. And she did work very hard."

Chapter **14** **Closing the Show**

The next morning, a meeting was held at Blaine-Thompson, the advertising agency that had been signed to promote _Johnny No-Trump_. Those present were, for the most part, the same people who had gathered at the bar next door to the Cort Theater during rehearsals: Mary Mercier, Joe Hardy, Charles Woodward, Richard Barr, and, in addition, Howard Atlee.

By now, the reviews from the afternoon papers, the _New York Post_ and the _Daily News,_ were available. These were scanned along with the _Times,_ and television and radio reviews, for favorable comments. Neither the _Post_ nor the _News_ had ecstatic quotes with which to emblazon an ad for _Johnny No-Trump._ One referred to a "well-chosen cast and fine direction," and the other said, "The performances are all good." But the _Post's_ overall view of _Johnny No-Trump_ was that it was "a worthy try but a disappointment," and the _Daily News_ was even more negative, calling the play "labored comedy most of the way."

Joe Hardy described the meeting to me later. "Dick Barr was angry at the critics and a little put out," he said. "And Woodward didn't want to keep it open at all, I think because he could save a lot of money that he had in it and transfer it to _Everything in the Garden_ (the next ABW Broadway production). They called Walter Kerr (theater critic for the Sunday *Times*) to see what he thought about the play. He said that he had already written his piece for the following Sunday, so it would have been two weeks before he wrote about *Johnny No-Trump*. They decided they couldn't afford to wait and see if he would be favorable.

"They had no advance sales and no stars," Hardy continued. "I was no name, even the stars were no names really. I mean they don't have any following. And they had hardly any tickets sold for Monday night."

For whatever reasons—and the motives of the producers were debated for months afterward—Barr and Woodward decided to close *Johnny No-Trump* after only one performance. "Mary and Dick Barr and I had lunch at Sardi's," Joe said, "and then went back to Barr's office and phoned the actors."

The cast, of course, had read or heard about the *Post* and *Daily News* reviews, and to those who were at all realistic, a long run for *Johnny No-Trump* must have seemed unlikely. Still, few plays close overnight, even with worse reviews, and to many in the cast the telephone call they received from Richard Barr that afternoon came as a shock.

"When Dick Barr called me on Monday," Pat Hingle said, "and told me 'We're closing the show,' I thought he was sort of preparing me. Saying that we didn't get such good reveiws so we would have to close. We talked for a while, and I asked him, 'Will you be down there tonight?' And he said, 'Yes, I guess so. But what do you have to go down for? You don't have to clean out your dressing room right away!' And I said, 'You mean we're not going to play *tonight?*' And he said, 'Yes, we've closed the show.' I couldn't believe it."

The swift closing came as a shock to me as well. At first I didn't want to talk about the closing, and I assumed others would feel the same. Better to forget the whole endeavor—all the hopes and excitement I had shared with the company. But on Tuesday I was sufficiently curious to call Mary Mercier. I was surprised to hear her sounding more defiant than defeated at the other end of the line. "I'm not committing suicide if that's what you mean," Mary said. "It's all economics. They have to have words like 'smash' and 'fabulous' to keep a play going."

But several plans apparently were afoot to produce the play again. "There were too many people who liked it, actors and theater people who didn't even bother to go to the opening night because they thought it would run. You should watch closely now," she added. "You haven't heard the end of this yet."

Mary Mercier was right. Far from wanting to forget *Johnny No-Trump,* everyone seemed eager to talk about it. It was as though, just by talking, they could keep it alive a little longer. What was unusual in the case of *Johnny No-Trump* was that the reaction went beyond those involved in the production. For a week or so after the show closed, Don Scardino received between twenty and thirty phone calls a day, and Mary Mercier received calls and letters for several weeks.

The abruptness of the closing was the cause of some of the indignation, and particularly incensed Mary's agent, Bertha Case. "Mary came in here on Monday," Bertha Case said, "looking very drawn and told me they were going to close the play. I thought she meant in a week or two but Mary said, 'No, they're not reopening tonight.' I said, 'You mean it's a *fait accompli?*' and she said it was, that they were calling the actors and telling them not to come back.

"I tried to call Dick Barr while Mary was in my office, but he wasn't in. But I called him later and told him what I thought. To say you love a play, and then as a producer not to give it one drop of blood! For a producer who likes writers, this is terrible! Dick Barr told me no one was buying tickets. And he said there weren't any lines from the reviews that could have been quoted. There *were* lines that could have been quoted, including the last line of Clive Barnes's review, saying that he would rather have written this play than *Cactus Flower.* I would even have quoted the last part of that line—'but that's not saying that it will run as long'—just to show them that it would."

Yet when I spoke with Richard Barr the day after he made his decision to close the play, he claimed that he had no alternative. "The play got extremely negative reviews," Barr said. "We had taken in forty-two dollars for Monday night, and I simply would not have actors perform before that kind of house."

Actually, the reviews of *Johnny No-Trump* were mixed. Pat Hingle estimated, after seeing mimeographed copies of them all, that there were as many good ones as bad. The radio reviews were generally positive, as were two of the television reviews. The *Wall Street Journal* said, "Miss Mercier has written perceptive and often amusing roles for her characters." The *Journal of Commerce* found *Johnny No-Trump* "good, straightforward theater, heartily recommended." On October 12, four days after the closing, the *Village Voice* reviewed the play: "*Johnny No-Trump* is possibly the most honest and unpretentious dramatization of the conflict between young and old Broadway will see this season . . . This one is well worth seeing."

"It's weird," Mary Mercier commented when she learned of the *Village Voice* review. "We seem to have cut it right down the middle. The big reviewers didn't like it and the small reviewers did. I wonder why that is?" Whatever the reason, few plays succeed without the approval of the big reviewers, particularly Clive Barnes.

Months later, I talked with Clive Barnes, a short chunky man with sideburns and warm brown eyes, about *Johnny No-Trump*. By that time, Barnes had reviewed a whole season of plays and dance concerts, yet it was obvious that *Johnny No-Trump* had particularly concerned him. I asked him, as we sat in the living room of his large apartment, if he would have written a different review if he had it to do over again.

"Well of course," he said brusquely. "One would always write any notice differently. Say you sent a letter last week. If you were going to write it today, it would be a different letter. But the basic thing of the review, I think, would have been the same. The actual phraseology, which can sometimes be important, would obviously vary.

"*Johnny No-Trump* was a play that to me showed a great deal of inexperience but it was a play by a talented writer who was trying to deal with real people in real situations. And although I think it was very much only partially successful, to write even a partially successful play is really an enormous achievement. And in fact some of the plays that are so-called hits are much worse than *Johnny No-Trump*. At the end of my review I noted that I would have preferred to have written this than to have written *Cactus Flower,* though the irony is that *Cactus Flower* survived for three years and *Johnny No-Trump* ran but one night.

"You know what happened. The play got not unfavorable notices. The notices would suggest that the play was interesting, promising, didn't entirely work out—these kinds of notices. But of course these were not the kind of notices that would produce a hit, and the next day the response at the box office was not enormous.

"I think this is a show that should have gone off-Broadway, where it would have stood a much better chance of finding an audience. If it had been done off-Broadway, union costs would have been less, the rent would have been less. It would have been possible to have kept it on for a bit and let it see if it couldn't find an audience.

"The whole story of *Johnny No-Trump* illustrated the way in which the economics of Broadway are so depressing at the moment. If the play isn't the biggest thing to hit the theater since tip-up seats, no one wants it. And this is a terribly bad atmosphere. People blame the critics, but the reason for this is really very clear. The reason is the terrible economic situation on Broadway. The unions demand enormous salaries. What's more, these theaters happen to be built on some of the most expensive chunks of land in the world. Because of the price of tickets, people don't want to see any show in the world, they want to see the greatest show. *Johnny No-Trump* is a typical example of the way a play suffers from this situation."

After talking with Clive Barnes, I realized that no one person was to blame for the swift closing of *Johnny No-Trump*. In the *Times* announcement of the closing, Richard Barr blamed the critics: "The fact that the critics did not appreciate that this play was so far above the level, both in writing and production, of almost any American play for the past several seasons indicates to me that there is a great struggle ahead for sensitive, intelligent, talented playwrights. We can't fight this lethargy on the part of the critics."

And on October 20, Clive Barnes wrote a piece about the Broadway season to date in which he blamed the producer. "This season, even this early, has regrets as well as its triumphs. Personally, I regret that *Johnny No-Trump,* not a brilliant but a promising play, superbly acted with a lovely cast, led by Pat Hingle, was abruptly taken off by its producer before it had a chance to get word-of-mouth resuscitation. This was Broadway at its most savage. Some plays need nursing, and *Johnny No-Trump* was a perfect example."

Yet, while some thought Barr brutal for closing so abruptly, another producer who had seen Mary Mercier's play and liked it said, "I would have done exactly the same thing in Barr's position. He had no choice. He could have kept the play open by papering the house, but it would have been an exercise in futility. You say it was hard on the actors and the playwright when the play closed overnight, but I'll tell you something that's even harder, and that's playing to forty or fifty people night after night. I've tried nursing a play before, and it's something I never want to go through again. You don't sleep, you worry night after night about what you can do, and there's absolutely nothing you can do."

If *Johnny No-Trump* deserved better, as many thought, it was what Clive Barnes and everyone else called the "situation" on Broadway that was at fault. And of all the comments, Walter Kerr's was the only one that proposed a remedy. He wrote an article that appeared in the *Times* two weeks after the closing, proposing a "tryout house," a theater of Broadway proportions where a play could be tried out before audiences at a minimum cost before going into full-scale production.

"I say that we are dying for such a playhouse," Kerr wrote, "because I have just seen a play die for lack of such a playhouse. Two weeks ago tonight, *Johnny No-Trump* opened at the Cort. It closed after a single performance. Being the first play of an unknown author and drawing only mildly friendly yes–no notices from the first night press, it had nowhere to stand—inexpensively—until it could discover how interested audiences might be in it.

"The damage done by the sudden closing—and sudden closings are multiplying furiously at the moment—was and is enormous. Beyond doubt, author Mary Mercier's confidence has been damaged: one-night runs suggest total ineptitude and are perforce humiliating. Worse, she has been cheated of experience: she hasn't even been able to learn much for her pains. Yet she *is*—or should have been—a discovery, she is plainly talented, she is already capable of a blunt and crackling speech that insists upon being listened to, of managing open and moving confrontations between scratchy, well-meaning, strong-willed people, of giving breath and resilience to the people themselves. Her structural gaucheries were almost unimportant; she has a voice."

Postscript

Don Scardino had never been able to stay away from the Cort theater for long, and on the Monday that *Johnny No-Trump* closed, he and his girlfriend dropped by just after noon to pick up a jacket. As Don hung his dressing room key on the rack near the stage door, Harry, the doorman, inquired if he had cleaned out his dressing room. Don asked Harry what he meant, and Harry told him the show was closing.

"I couldn't believe it," Don said. "I went out onstage in a daze. Everything looked normal. The set was still there. But I really started to believe it when I saw Michael Kasden walking up the aisle with thirty programs under his arm. I thought, 'What is he doing with those programs if the show isn't closing?' I asked him, 'Michael, is it true?' He said he was really sorry, and that he didn't want me to find out this way.

"Up until opening night," Don said, "I'd been sort of dreaming and waiting and hoping, but not hoping too much for fear I'd be disappointed. And then, at the party, when we got those marvelous reviews and that girl was there taking pictures, it all seemed to be coming true. Then after that everything went downhill. The television reviews got worse and then the *Times* review came."

At first Don was "too stunned to react. I walked out of the theater, collapsed on the fire escape, and cried. I put my girlfriend in a cab. It was like a death, and you felt you wanted to be with the people involved, like you do when someone dies.

"I couldn't tell you before what I learned from Joe Hardy," Don said, "but I realize now that he taught me honesty. I became an actor under him. Up until then, I'd only been a performer. It had never really happened to me before.

"The last scene of the play, when I hear that my mother's dead, didn't really start working until about two nights before the opening. Up until then it still didn't have the ring of truth, it was missing maybe ten percent. And I remember Joe called me onstage before the second to last preview and said, 'Nobody's ever died on you, have they?' And I said no, because I've never had any close friend or relative die. And Joe asked me if I'd ever gotten really furious. And I said rarely, because it's not part of my nature. So Joe said, 'Suppose you were in a room full of older people and every time you said something, somebody hit you, belted you right in the gut so hard that it sickened you?' That night, the death happened to me for the first time. You probably saw it. Joe had told me to take my time and look around the house and see the house. And that night I looked around, and touched the desk and said, 'She was just in the room. She was there. Right there,' and it happened.

"But when it really happened to me, it was too late. That was when I went back to the theater on Monday and found out the play had closed after one performance. It was like the last scene. 'She was just in the room. She was there. Right there.' It hurt me so much to think I'd never walk down those stairs again. When I saw Joe, I told him that I knew how to play the last scene. I'd never had anyone die on me before. Now I had."

On Monday evening several of the actors cleared out their dressing rooms. On Tuesday, two days after opening night, the set was disassembled. Once again the Cort stage was bare.

Bibliography

The following bibliography offers suggestions for further reading about the theater. All of the books listed are currently in print. An asterisk (*) marks those available in paperback.

Practical Books

Probably the most instructive books on ACTING are those of the great Russian teacher and director, Constantin Stanislavski. *An Actor Prepares* (New York: Theater Arts, 1969), is so rich in helpful techniques for the actor that it can be returned to again and again. *Strasberg at the Actors Studio,* edited by Robert H. Hethmon (New York: The Viking Press, 1965), is a selection from tape-recorded sessions Lee Strasberg has conducted at the Actors Studio. In focusing on the acting problems of Studio members, Strasberg gives lucid, usable advice to actors in general. Interviews with actors deal less directly with the actor's craft, but they too can be helpful. *Lillian and Helen Ross, *The Player: A Profile of an Art* (New York: Simon and Schuster, 1962), is a collection of brief, revealing interviews with over fifty actors and actresses. Interviews in greater depth can be found in *Lewis Funke and John E. Booth, *Actors Talk About Acting* (New York: Avon Books, 1967), and *Great Acting* (New York: Hill and Wang, 1967). The latter is the published version of interviews conducted on television with seven of England's greatest actors and actresses and includes a photographic review of each performer's career.

The most useful introduction to DIRECTING is probably *Directors on Directing,* edited by Toby Cole and Helen Krich Chinoy (Indianapolis: The Bobbs-Merrill Co. Inc., 1963). Particularly valuable is the third section of the book, "The Director at Work." Here are collected the notes and thoughts of great directors concerning their work on specific plays.

The art of PLAYWRITING is discussed in essays and working notes by such great American playwrights as Tennessee Williams and Eugene O'Neill in *American Playwrights on Drama,* edited by Horst Frens (New York: Hill and Wang, 1965). *The Playwrights Speak,* edited by Walter Wager (New York: Dell Publishing Co., 1968), a collection of interviews with contemporary playwrights, also casts light on the dramatist's creative process.

Michael Warre, *Designing and Making Stage Scenery* (New York: Reinhold Book Corp., 1966), is both a compact history of SET DESIGN and a practical guide to set-building. For more detailed help with set construction, there is *F. A.

Buerki, *Stagecraft for Nonprofessionals* (Madison: The University of Wisconsin Press, 1966).

Bert Gruver, *The Stage Manager's Handbook* (New York: Harper and Brothers, 1953), is a useful manual on STAGE MANAGING. The mechanics of PRODUCING are dealt with lucidly in two books by Donald C. Farber: *From Option to Opening: A Guide for the Off-Broadway Producer* (New York: DBS Publications, Inc., 1968), and *Producing on Broadway* (New York: DBS Publications, Inc., 1969).

Jean Dalrymple, *Careers and Opportunities in the Theater* (E. P. Dutton, 1969), is a useful guide for anyone seeking work in the theater.

History and Biography

An excellent HISTORY of the drama is Bamber Gascoigne, *World Theater: An Illustrated History* (Boston: Little Brown and Co., 1968), a large volume which traces theater history from its beginnings to the present in pictures as much as in words. There is also *Kenneth MacGowan and William Melnitz, *Golden Ages of the Theater* (New Jersey: Prentice Hall, 1959). Brooks Atkinson, *Broadway* (New York: The Macmillan Co., 1970). is a pleasant history of theater on Broadway. For a detailed look at each theater season, in New York and regional theater, there is *The Burns Mantle Theater Yearbook* (New York: Dodd, Mead & Co.), which has appeared every year since 1919. The most recent edition, for example, includes synopses of ten plays (chosen by editor Otis L. Guernsey Jr. as the best on and off-Broadway), photographs and summaries of the season in regional U.S. theaters and in London. The black artist's struggle to be seen and heard is related in *Loften Mitchell, *Black Drama: The Story of the American Negro in the Theatre* (New York: Hawthorn Books, Inc., 1967).

BIOGRAPHIES by or about theater people are abundant. Two excellent ones, diametrically opposed in mood, are *Moss Hart, *Act One* (New York: Signet, 1959), an exuberant autobiographical view of the years leading up to this playwright's first Broadway hit, and *Arthur and Barbara Gelb, *O'Neill* (New York: Dell Publishing Co., Inc., 1965), an absorbing account of playwright Eugene O'Neill's stormy life. The paperback version has been abridged by the authors.

*William Redfield, *Letters from an Actor* (New York: The Viking Press, 1969), is an amusing journal, written by an actor in a minor role, of rehearsals of *Hamlet,* starring Richard Burton and directed by John Gielgud.

Glossary

Apron   The part of the stage in front of the main curtain.

Arena Stage   See **Stage.**

Audition   To perform for those casting a play, with the purpose of getting a part.

Backers   Investors in a play. Sometimes called "angels."

Backstage   The portion of the theater behind the acting area, including dressing rooms, etc.

Battens

Pipe. Lengths of pipe to which lights, flats or curtains are fastened, then hoisted into place.

Wooden. Lengths of lumber used as the framework for cloth scenery.

Bit Part   A very small part.

Blocking   Stage movement worked out between the actors and director during rehearsals.

Box Set   An interior setting with three walls and, often, a ceiling.

Bridge   A narrow platform located high above the stage floor and built to accommodate spotlights and other lighting units. Usually it is designed as a catwalk, where the electrician can adjust and set lights.

Broadway   A major north-south street in New York City. Also, a group of 34 theaters located on and near Broadway in midtown Manhattan, all of which seat at least 800 theatergoers.

Business, Stage   Any physical actions of minor import performed on the stage.

Call   Used as a noun to refer to the work schedule or "call" for the following day, week, etc.

Call Board   Bulletin board backstage where rehearsal schedules, etc., are posted.

Characterization   Whatever the actor adds to or changes in his everyday manner and personality to create a role.

Cue   Any occurrence, such as the last words of a speech or piece of business, which signals someone onstage or backstage to proceed to the next line or action.

Cyc (Cyclorama)   A backdrop, either temporary or permanent, which is used to simulate the sky.

Dimmer   Any of the many different devices which control the intensity of stage lights.

Dress Rehearsals   Final rehearsals of a play before opening night. Ideally, the set should be finished, lights adjusted and costumes complete for these rehearsals.

Dressing a Set   Adding small things—pictures, curtains, tablecloth—which make a set look lived in.

Drop   Large expanses of material which are "dropped" (batten at top, weight at bottom) behind a scene and painted for desired effect.

Escape Stairs   Everything that goes up must come down, and that includes actors exiting from "upstairs" doors. The escape stairs are on the backstage side of these doors and allow the actor to go back to his dressing room during long breaks.

Equity   Actors' Equity Association, the stage actors' union.

Exterior   An out-of-doors setting.

Extras   Actors, or just people off the street, used to fill up crowd scenes.

Featherbedding   Union rulings which require management to hire unneeded personnel.

Flat   The most basic component of stage scenery. A wooden frame, of varying size and shape, covered with material suitable for painting.

Flies (Fly Loft)   The space above the stage used for flying scenery.

Fly   To elevate scenery by means of ropes, pulleys or a counterweight system.

Footlights   A trough of lights in the floor immediately in front of the curtain.

Gel (Gelatine)   Transparent, colored sheets made of animal jelly and used to give lights different colors.

Heavy   Slang for "the bad guy."

Hit   In the commercial theater, a show which is making a profit.

Hold Book   To act as prompter during rehearsals or performances.

House   The auditorium or the audience.

House Lights   The lights used to illuminate the auditorium, as distinct from those both in the auditorium and above the stage which illuminate the stage.

Improvisation   Actors inventing the scene as they go along.

Making the Rounds   Going to auditions, open calls, producers' and agents' offices, in search of a job in the theater.

Marquee   A canopy over the sidewalk in front of a theater, often used to advertise the play or movie showing within.

Mask   *v.* To make use of flats, curtains, etc., in order to obscure offstage areas from the audience's view.

Method   In phrases such as "the method," or "method acting" this word refers to the acting approach employed by Constantin Stanislavski, the great Russian teacher and director, or his followers. Stanislavski's ideas reflected the movement toward realism which occurred at the turn of the century in the work of such playwrights as Chekhov and Ibsen. His teachings helped actors to avoid stylized, artificial acting by working from their own experience and emotions in creating a role.

Notices   Reviews.

Offstage   The stage area outside the confines of the setting or acting area.

Off-Broadway This term is defined by Equity as referring to any theater of less than 300 seats in Manhattan but outside the area bounded by Fifth and Ninth Avenues, from 34th Street to 56th Street, and by Fifth Avenue and the Hudson River from 56th Street to 72nd Street. Off-Broadway also tends to be less expensive to both producer and theatergoer than Broadway and more experimental.

Option A legal term referring to a producer's exclusive purchased right to present a certain play within a certain time.

Out Front This phrase refers to the "front" or auditorium of the theater, and thus describes the vantage point of anyone who watches rehearsals from there, i.e. the producers, the playwright, etc.

Paper the House To hand out free tickets in order to at least partially fill a theater.

Portal A gate, door or entrance. Also a temporary proscenium set within a permanent one.

Previews Performances prior to the official opening.

Project *v.* To enlarge voice and movement so that they reach the rear of the auditorium. Projection is essential on the stage, but often ridiculous in TV and movies where the viewer is right up next to the actor's image.

Prompter The person who follows the script during rehearsals and performances, and gives the actors lines when necessary.

Properties (Props) Pieces used in the action of the play which are too small to qualify as scenery.

Proscenium Arch The frame separating the stage from the auditorium on a proscenium stage.

Proscenium Stage See **Stage.**

Regional Theater Theater, particularly year-round professional theater, outside New York.

Repertory Company A permanent acting company which presents their "repertoire" of plays in rotation through a season, as opposed to a stock company which performs a play for a set period of time, then goes on to the next play without returning to the first.

Revolving Stage A disk which is either built into the stage floor or on top of it, on which several box sets may be placed and rotated into position. One of several devices for quick scene changes.

Road Show Generally refers to the touring version of a Broadway or off-Broadway success.

Royalty The writer's percentage of the profits from his work. On Broadway the Dramatists Guild contract requires that the playright receive at least 5% of the first $5,000 of gross weekly box office receipts, plus 7½% of the next $2,000 plus 10% of the receipts over $7,000.

Run Length of time a play stays open.

Run-Through The rehearsal of a scene, act, or entire play without interruption.

Scrim A loosely woven material resembling cheesecloth, used for window glass onstage and for special effects. Lit from behind, the scrim becomes transparent. Lit from the front it is opaque.

Set The set is the stage environment designed and built for a specific play. Also, as a verb, "set" means to freeze stage business, lines, etc.

Spike Marks Marks put on floor to give exact position of furniture or set.

Stage The acting area of a theater. Increasingly in recent years, stages are being designed in a variety of shapes, some of which are the following:

Arena stage. Acting area surrounded on all sides by the audience.

Flexible stage. Area equipped with movable seats, and therefore open to an unlimited number of audience-stage arrangements.

Proscenium stage. The most common type of stage everywhere from high schools to Broadway. The stage is separated from the auditorium by a rectangular arch, with a varying amount of apron out in front of it.

Thrust stage. Like the stage in Shakespeare's time, this acting area thrusts out into the auditorium and the seating is arranged around it in a horseshoe shape.

Stage Crew Those who work backstage during a production, including the following:

Stage manager. Sets up stage for all rehearsals, records blocking and business, oversees myriad daily rehearsal problems. After the show opens, he is in complete charge of all performances, can call special rehearsals for understudies, etc.

Assistant Stage Manager. Often holds book, in addition to helping stage manager in other areas.

Master Electrician. In charge of putting in lights, running lights during performances, and striking lights.

Assistant electricians.

Master carpenter. In charge of bringing in, repairing and striking set.

Flymen. Stagehands who handle ropes.

Grips. Stagehands who move scenery.

Production propertyman. In charge of procuring props.

Property crew. In charge of laying out props for the actors and striking them.

Stage Directions For the purpose of planning stage movements, the stage is divided into five main areas: *upstage,* which is the area at the back of the stage, farthest from the audience; *downstage,* which is closest to the audience; *stage right,* the area on the actor's right as he faces the audience; *stage left,* the area on the actor's left as he faces the audience; and *center stage,* right in the middle of the stage. The director may combine several of these stage directions, as in "down right" or "up right center."

Stage Manager See **Stage Crew.**

Staging Blocking.

Star Generally, any very famous actor is thought of as a star, but the working definition for Broadway contracts is any person whose name appears above the title of the show or who has "starring" or "also starring" before his name.

Stock Company A company of actors who prepare a play, present it for a period of time, then present another. Differs from a repertory company, which rotates plays. In the United States, "stock" often refers to summer stock, which functions similarly during the summer months.

Strike To remove. To "strike" a set is to remove the set and everything on it from the stage.

Switchboard The control board for stage lights.

Tech Rehearsal The first dress rehearsal, during which the concentration is on technical problems, including lighting, sound levels, and costumes.

Thrust Stage See **Stage.**

Trap A removable section of the stage floor, through which actors can appear or disappear.

Traveler The track used for hanging draw curtains. Also the curtains themselves.

Tryout (Out-of-Town Tryout) Performances in one or several major American cities prior to New York opening.

Understudy Actor hired to learn lines of one or more cast members and replace same if illness, etc., makes it necessary.

Upstaging Moving upstage, and thereby forcing the actor playing opposite to turn his back on the audience. Not likely to win an audience or fellow-actors.

Wings Offstage area beyond audience sightlines.

The Author: Sue Jacobs now lives in Boston with her husband, a psychiatrist, and two young children. She grew up in southern Ohio and performed in plays and musicals while an undergraduate at Oberlin College in Oberlin, Ohio. While in college, she spent a summer performing with the Oberlin Gilbert and Sullivan Players on Cape Cod. Following graduation she spent two seasons acting, singing and working backstage at the Cleveland Playhouse, a professional repertory company in Cleveland. While still in Cleveland, she worked as a newspaper reporter on a suburban daily. She and her family moved to New York in 1966, and lived in Manhattan at the time *Johnny No-Trump* opened on Broadway. Mrs. Jacobs is currently at work on a second book about an underground film, made in Ann Arbor, Michigan during the summer of 1970.

Text set in Times Roman. Composed, printed and bound by The Book Press, Brattleboro, Vermont. Typography by Thomas Morley.